OTHER BOOKS BY P. CRAIG RUSSELL

OPERA

P. CRAIG RUSSELL

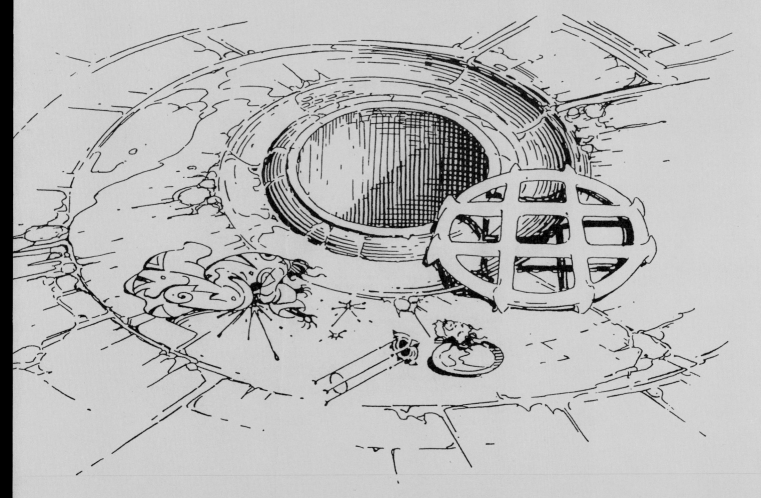

ECLIPSE BOOKS

Published by
Eclipse Books
Post Office Box 1099
Forestville, California 95436

First edition, 1990

10 9 8 7 6 5 4 3 2 1

Trade Paperback: ISBN 0-913035-53-X
Signed, Limited Edition Hardcover: ISBN 0-913035-56-4

Published simultaneously in Spain by Toutain Editor

Editor: Catherine Yronwode
Design: Rian Hughes, Titan Studios

Library of Congress Cataloging-in-Publication Data

Russell, P. Craig
    Opera/P. Craig Russell. —1st ed.
    Contents: Parsifal—Salomé—Mahler—Pelléas & Mélisande.
    ISBN 0-913035-56-54. —ISBN 0-913035-53-X (pbk)
    1. Operas—Comic books, strips, etc. 2. Songs with orchestra
—Comic books, strips, etc.
ML89.R93 1990
782.1'026'9—dc20   90-38657
                                          CIP MN

CONTENTS

PARSIFAL

INTRODUCTION

Li Contes del Graal (The Legend of the Grail) was written about 1175 by that
champion of Arthurian romance, Chrétien de Troyes. He adapted his narrative
from a book about the Knights of the Round Table lent to him by the warrior,
Philip of Alsace, who fought in England about 1172. Chrétien's 9234 line
fragment about Sir Perceval engaged the attention of Wolfram von
Eschenbach, who composed his *Parzifal* on this chilvalric theme in the early
1200s. His poem stands as the noblest literary achievement of the Middle Ages,
with the sole exception of Dante's *Divine Comedy*. *Parzifal* is unique in its
construction, its vivid language, and its implications both philosophical
and sociological.

The renunciation of worldly pleasures and adherence to love above lust are
ideas which have occupied the minds of artists in and out of Medieval clothing.
No exception was Richard Wagner (1813-83), the German opera composer and
the most controversial figure of his time. He made the conflict between flesh
and spirit the main theme in six of his seven mature works. His most tragic
characters all cry out for release from their greed and imperfection, to an
unselfish love.

This present story is adapted from the second act of Wagner's last work,
Parsifal. It follows Wagner's script closely, with one important change. The
role of 'redeemer' given to Parsifal by Wagner presents no problem if the story
is entirely fictional. But, because *Parsifal* deals with the historical figure of
Christ, who in Wagner's work is relegated to a symbol, the Grail then becomes
further removed, being a symbol of a symbol, thus robbing the message of its
power. If the fate of the individual turns upon our inability to raise ourselves to
the level of an all-loving, all-knowing God-likeness, then why should Parsifal,
the mortal, be any different?

In this version it is only as he is chosen, tried, enlightened, and finally, blessed,
that Parsifal can extend the strength God gives him through the 'true
redeemer', Jesus, to an affirmation of responsible love and the resultant
destruction of evil, here symbolized by Klingsor.

Partrick C. Mason

A FU-TUNE KARMIX PRESENTATION

Art-Visual Direction
P. Craig Russell

Story Adaptation Script
Patrick C. Mason

Adapted from the opera by
Richard Wagner

Lettering:
Orzechowski & Kawecki

PARSIFAL
PART I: HIS JOURNEY

PARSIFAL WANDERED MANY LONG DAYS AFTER LEAVING THE HOLY GROUND OF MONSALVAT, ITS RITES AND MYSTRIES STILL IN HIS FOOLISH HEAD. PARSIFAL, THE **CHIEF** OF FOOLS, WAS STILL STRICKEN WITH THE MEMORY OF THE SUFFERING **AMFORTAS**, GUARDIAN OF THE GRAIL AND PRIEST OF THE KNIGHTLY BROTHER-HOOD AT HIS SACRED MOUNTAIN FORTRESS... BUT PARSIFAL KNEW **THIS** REMEMBRANCE WOULD VANISH LIKE ALL THE OTHERS... ALL, THAT IS, BUT **ONE**:

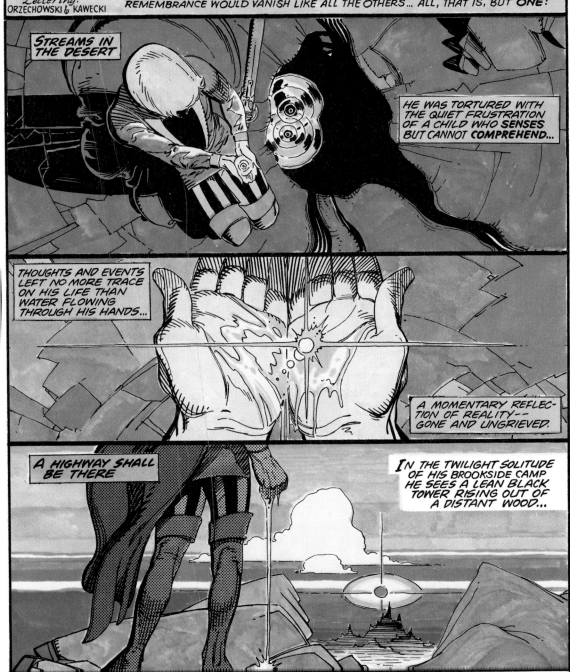

HE CLIMBS UP A NARROW BANK ONTO THE SURROUNDING BANKS AND STARES INTO THE SUN. HOW MANY YEARS HAS IT BEEN SINCE HE LEFT HIS HOME? HE DOES NOT KNOW -- THE WORLD BEING ONLY AN OPENING OF POSSIBILITIES TO

HIM, EACH ONE FURTHER FROM REGRET. BUT **ONE** MEMORY TIME HAS NEVER ERASED: HIS MOTHER -- WHERE **IS** SHE? WHY HAD HE **LEFT** HER? THIS QUESTION, INDEED, DRIVES HIM TO LEAVE ALL THE REST BEHIND...

...PURSUING DREAMS AT NIGHT, LIKE A LOST GHOST-CHILD.

AWAY FROM THE STREAM, THE AIR IS DRY--HIS FACE DRAWS TIGHT...

... BUT HIS MIND DRAWS TIGHTER, HESITATING...

...HESITATING ON THE BRINK OF A DESERT SO VAST THAT IT COULD NOT BE BORNE, EXCEPT FOR THE DARK WOOD WHICH OFFERS REFUGE. THE OMINOUS STRUCTURE RISING FROM THE WOOD'S MURKY MIDST PIERCES THE SETTING SUN AND BLOODIES THE HORIZON.

THE FOOL TURNS FROM THE SHELTER OF THE STREAM, GLADLY FORSAKING HIS PAST TO FOLLOW THE **YEARNING** WHICH QUICKENS HIS WEARY STEPS...

... THE YEARNING WHICH IS THE ONLY ALTERNATIVE TO HIS CONFUSION...

BUT IT IS A **HEARTLESS** YEARNING. HE FLEES FROM THE THOUGHT OF AMFORTAS' SUFFERING, FLEEING FROM THE PITY AND WISDOM DEMANDED OF HIS FOOLISH, YOUNG HEART.

THE SUN SETS BEFORE HIM

THE MOON RISES, UNNOTICED AT HIS BACK

THE ROAMING OF A WIND-DRIVEN SOUL OFTEN SERVES TO LEAD THAT SOUL TO EVENTUAL REST, THOUGH IT BE ALL UNKNOWN IN THE WANDERING. JUST SO, THE VALIANT BOY GOES ON--HEEDLESS OF THE DEEPENING NIGHT AND LEAGUES OF DUST DISTURBED OVER A BARREN LAND--ON INTO AN AP-POINTED ENCOUNTER OF WHICH HE REMAINS UNAWARE. WEARY AND SLOW OF STEP, HE ARRIVES AT THE FOREST'S EDGE.

TWO PINES RISE BEFORE HIM, A GATE TO A LAND THAT STANDS OPPOSED TO THE DESERT BEYOND ITS BORDERS.

FROM FORGETFULNESS TO THE UNKNOWN HIS PATH IS OPEN. THE FOOL STANDS PERPLEXED, BUT SENSES SOME DIM HOPE IN HIS PERPLEXITY.

...AND HERE IN THIS DARK WOOD I CHOOSE TO SEEK MY EN-LIGHTENMENT?

HIS DESPAIR IS STRONG BUT HIS YEARNING HEART IS ADAMANT...

...AND THAT ALONE MAKES HIM TURN FROM THE STARLIT EASTERN SKY

11

THE COOLNESS OF THE FOREST RELIEVES THE CONFUSED TRAVELLER AND HOURS PASS SILENTLY AS HE FOLLOWS HIS SHADOW DOWN THE PATH, ILLUMINATED BY THE MOON'S FRAGILE LIGHT.

THE GROUND, COVERED WITH MOSS AND DEAD LEAVES, CUSHIONS HIS FEET AND GIVES STRENGTH TO HIS BODY.

A MAGIC STILLNESS-- NIGHT'S OWN SPELL-- GLADDENS HIM, AND PARSIFAL SITS ON A LARGE ROCK TO VIEW THE SPLENDOR, BOTH

INNOCENT AND VOLUPTUOUS. THE SILENCE IS COMPLETE BUT FOR THE WIND. IT WHISTLES--NO, IT IS SINGING! HE LIES IN A HALF-SLEEP AS THE LADY OF THE TREES SINGS TO HIM--AS THE WIND SIGHS THROUGH THE WOODS. A SMALL MELANCHOLY CREEPS OVER HIM AND... HE **SEES** HER! A GREY, MIST-FILLED VISION... SINGS...

Silvered kisses placed I on his brow,
Long we watched the glowing in the night!
Long we filled each other with our eyes.
So now, I long to hold
him in my sight.

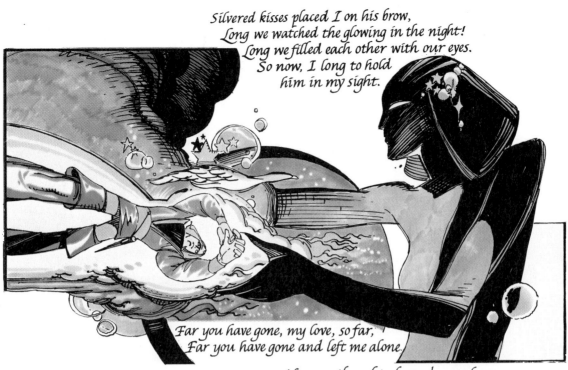

Far you have gone, my love, so far,
Far you have gone and left me alone.

Never a thought of me do you have,
And yet, you will return!

HE LAY ON THE ROCK, FEELING THE ROCK AND
LISTENING TO "THE LADY".

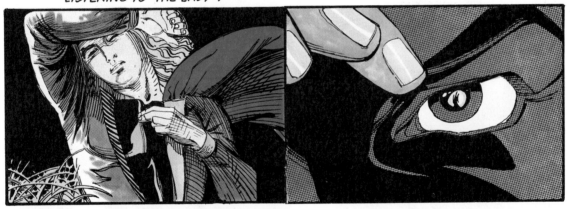

HE DOES NOT WISH TO WAKE FROM HIS REVERIE
BUT IS TEMPTED TO OPEN HIS EYES...

...AND AS HE DOES, THE VOICE AND THE
VISION DISSOLVE IN THE WIND.

PARSIFAL SEES THE TOWER
QUITE CLOSE AND WITHOUT
COMPARE IN THE MOONLIGHT-
FLOODED NIGHT.

THE QUIET PAIN STILL IN HIS CHEST, HE CONTINUES WESTWARD--HIS DIMINISHING SHADOW THE ONLY EVIDENCE OF TIME'S EXISTENCE. NIGHT SEEMS ETERNAL-- BLISSFULLY SO.

AND THEN...

HE SEES A GLINT OF LIGHT ON THE PATH FAR AHEAD

HE HESITATES...

THEN RUNS FURIOUSLY TO THE SPOT BEYOND HIM AS IT SHINES BRIGHTER WITH EVERY STRIDE. FROM MANY YARDS PARSIFAL SEES THAT IT IS METAL...AND ROUND... A COIN!

AS HE BENDS OVER IT HE BLOCKS THE MOONLIGHT WHICH THE COIN REFLECTS.

THE MOON ABOVE HIM SENDS ITS COOL LIGHT DIRECTLY INTO HIS OPEN HANDS WHERE GLOWS THE COIN WHICH IS MARKED WITH A SYMBOL OF THAT SILVER ORB, CATCHING THE BEAMS OF THE OBJECT IT GLORIFIES.

HE IS HYPNOTIZED BY THE GLIMMER AND FILLED WITH A GREAT RUSH AND SWELL OF JOY.

HIS EYES RISE FROM THE LIGHT IN HIS PALM-- AND *THERE*...

THERE LIES A *GARDEN!* IT IS AS IF HIS JOY IS TRANSFORMED INTO SCENT AND SOUND AND THE MUTED COLOR OF A MOONLIT PARADISE OF FLOWERS AND VINES.

HE STANDS ALONE AND TRANSFIXED, LIKE ADAM IN *ANOTHER* GARDEN, WHEN HE THEN FEELS THE LARGER BLOSSOMS *MOVING*.

YOU HAVE FOUND ONE OF OUR COINS FOR US?

15

...WHERE HE LIES DOWN IN SWEET, BLISSFUL REST. THEN HE REMEMBERS THE COIN...

...BUT HE FEELS IT TIGHT IN HIS HAND AND SMILES.

SHE VIEWS HER PREY, SO DELIGHTFULLY PREPARED FOR HER.

KUNDRY WANTS HIM... ALONE.

YOU MUST LEAVE HIM TO ME NOW.

'TIS A PITY FOR ONE SO HANDSOME.

SURELY, KUNDRY APPROVES OF OUR WORK, SISTERS.

YES, DEAR ONES, BUT MINE IS A TASK FAR BEYOND YOUR POWERS.

AND BREAKING HIS TRANCE, SHE CALLS HIM...

PARSIFAL ...

MY NAME...

...AS ONCE MY MOTHER SPOKE IT...

...AND WHO...

...WHO ARE YOU? AND WHERE ARE THE OTHER FLOWERS... I MEAN...

THE CHILDREN OF THE GARDEN ARE BUT SERVANTS WHOM I DISMISSED. THEY WERE NO LONGER USEFUL HERE, BUT AS FOR YOU...

17

PARSIFAL

PART II: HIS TEMPTATION

KLINGSOR TURNS FROM THE TWO CAUGHT IN HIS TRAP-- TEMPTRESS AND VICTIM ALIKE CAUGHT IN HIS TWISTED NECROMANTIC NET. THE MAD WIZARD EXULTS IN HIS COMING TRIUMPH.

SHE SERVES ME WELL, THE WITCH! AND BY MY SPELLS SHE WILL 'EDUCATE' THIS YOUNG FOOL. Ha,ha! THE KNIGHTS SO PURE, THEY ALL WILL BE MADE WISE IN HER DEVILISH EMBRACE -- THEY ARE CONSUMPTIVES OF THE SOUL, LONGING ONLY FOR DEATH IN THEIR WEARY DOCTRINES OF RENUNCIATION.

I, TOO, ONCE CAST MY DELUDED, YOUTHFUL FANCY BEYOND MANKIND AND CREATED A CREATOR! THE HOME OF THE KNIGHTS OF THE GRAIL HARBOURED MY HUNGRY SPIRIT, FEEDING IT WITH POISONOUS RITUAL AND SUBSERVIANCE.

BUT I WAS EAGER FOR PLEASURE AND WAS FAR TOO CLEVER FOR THAT WOMANISH BROOD OF DOLTS! I SHOULD HAVE KNOWN ALL THEIR TALK OF THE SOUL AND THE SOUL'S PEACE TO BE INSANITY-- THE GRAIL IS THE SYMBOL OF THEIR EMPTY FAITH!

20

LEAVE MONSALVAT TONIGHT AND REPENT IN PRAYER AND FASTING.

REPENT? AFTER I HAD TAKEN THE FIRST STEP TO REAL FREEDOM?

NO, AMFORTAS, MY HOLY CLOWN!

PENANCE I DID, BUT NOT TO YOUR GOD! IN THE DARK CAVES OF MAGICIANS DID I BEND MY KNEE, MASTERING THE DIREST INCANTATIONS OF ALCHEMY AND NECROMANCY!

OH, WHAT A WORLD OF PROFIT AND DELIGHT OF POWER AND HONOR IS PROMISED TO THE STUDIOUS ARTISAN.

POWER I HAVE, AND A KINGDOM IN WHICH TO WIELD IT, A SPLENDID MOCKERY OF THAT MOUNTAIN GRAVEYARD OF DAMNED AMFORTAS.

MY GARDEN HOLDS RARE BLOSSOMS TO ENTICE THE KNIGHTS WHO WOULD APPROACH ME —

AND WITH THE WITCH KUNDRY AT MY CALL I NEED NOT FEAR EVEN THE STRONGEST OF THEM!

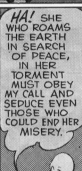

HA! SHE WHO ROAMS THE EARTH IN SEARCH OF PEACE, IN HER TORMENT MUST OBEY MY CALL AND SEDUCE EVEN THOSE WHO COULD END HER MISERY.

AND THE FALLEN ONES SHALL ONE DAY STORM MONSALVAT ITSELF!

AH! TO LOOK AMFORTAS IN THE FACE AGAIN.

AND RELIVE WITH HIM HIS SHAMEFUL BURDEN!

WOMAN, YOU SPEAK HIS NAME! WHERE DOES KLINGSOR HIDE? AND WHERE ARE THE LOST BRETHREN...

WHY TRAVEL FURTHER, WEARY MAN? THE WICKED ONE'S CASTLE I SHALL SHOW IN THE MORNING. REST HERE WHERE I MAY SOOTH YOUR TROUBLED HEART.

21

BUT -- FERRIS, SIR GAWAIN -- THEY'VE BEEN GONE FOR... MONTHS... WHAT IF... THEY'VE...

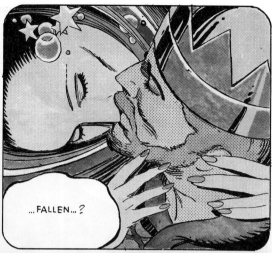

...FALLEN...?

AUURRRGH

AMFORTAS' COMPANION, PARTED FROM HIM BY KLINGSOR'S MAGIC, TURNS TOWARD THE KING'S CRY...

MASTER!!

IN CHRIST'S NAME, BE GONE, YE DEVILS!

HAHAHAHAHAH

HAHAHAHAHAHAHA!

YES, YOU'VE ESCAPED ME, BUT THIS SPEAR, ONCE SO PRECIOUS TO YOU-- THE SPEAR THAT PIERCED YOUR SAVIOR'S SIDE-- IT LEAVES DEEP WOUNDS THAT NEVER CLOSE. YOU RULE AS A PRIEST, BUT THEY ALL KNOW YOU AS A SICK AND FALLEN MAN, UNWORTHY OF YOUR OFFICE.

EVEN NOW YOU HOPE FOR DELIVERANCE, AS TOLD YOU IN A VISION... DELIVERANCE BY THE HANDS OF A *"PURE FOOL"*.

THERE HE STANDS, THE ONE APPOINTED TO END YOUR DISGRACE...

...BUT YOU HOPE IN VAIN! GO ON, *KING!* SACRIFICE YOURSELF AND YOUR BROTHERS TO SOME MEANINGLESS FUTURE -- BUT I SHALL SEE THAT BOY AT MY FEET! I SHALL SEE HIM BINDING YOU, PRIEST, FOR TORTURE! I SHALL RULE YOU *ALL WHEN AT LAST I HAVE* THE **GRAIL!**

23

NIGHT: THE MAGIC OF *KUNDRY'S* VOICE AND HER AGELESS CHARMS SOON DRAW THE VEIL OF IGNORANCE FROM *PARSIFAL* WHICH HE HAS LEARNED TO ACCEPT.

FOR, WHAT BROUGHT YOU HERE IF NOT THE DESIRE TO KNOW?

HE PRESSES THE COIN IN HIS HAND. ITS COOLNESS REMINDS HIM OF HER VOICE AND HE SENSES, WITH TERROR, THE IRRESISTIBLE SORCERY WHICH MAKES HIM TRUST HER.

FROM WHERE HAVE YOU COME, LADY, THAT YOU KNOW MY NAME AND JOURNEY?

FAR AWAY IS MY HOME, AND MUCH HAVE I SEEN. I SAW THE CHILD ON HIS MOTHER'S BREAST. I HEARD HIS FIRST LAUGHTER AS *HERZELEIDE* POURED OUT HER LOVE TO THE BABE.

AND I SAW THE TEAR WHICH HE DID *NOT* SEE AS HER HEART, FULL OF AFFLICTION, YEARNED FOR HIS FATHER, *GAMURET*, GONE TO KNIGHTLY COMBAT IN THE NORTH!

MY FATHER... *GAMURET*...

24

SO FEARFUL WAS SHE OF THE SON FOLLOWING THE FATHER THAT SHE KEPT HIM FROM THOUGHTS OF BATTLE, AND THE HONOUR OF VICTORY.

YET, WOMAN, I AM A FIGHTER! A GOOD ONE!

PARSIFAL, YOU SHALL SEE -- AND BELIEVE. LOOK INTO THE COIN AND LEARN THAT WHICH YOU HAVE CHOSEN TO FORGET.

THE COIN, WHICH GAINED HIM ENTRANCE TO THE GARDEN, NOW GLOWS WITH THE COLORS OF A FAMILIAR LAND, ONE YET FAR AWAY.

AS PARSIFAL STARES INTO ITS BRIGHT- NESS HE SEES A CHILD IN IDLE PLAY, UNAWARE OF A CHARGER SWIFTLY APPROACHING. OH, IF HE COULD ONLY WARN THE CHILD OF THE DANGER HE IS ABOUT TO...

WHOA

CHILD, WHY DO YOU HIDE IN THE OPEN PATH WHEN YONDER THICKET WOULD CONCEAL YOU SAFELY?

25

MY
FATHER
DEAD...

MY
MOTHER
DESERTED...

O
CRUEL
WISDOM
THAT
REVEALS
THIS TO
ME!

YOUR
MOTHER...
WOULD YOU
SEE HER
AGAIN?

AGAIN
THE COIN GLOWS--
THIS TIME
WITH THE
SOFT COLOR OF
TWILIGHT.

THE LADY HERZELEIDE
STANDS, PALE AND WORN,
IN THE HALF-DOORWAY
OF THE FORSAKEN
HOUSE AT SUNSET AS
SHE HAS DONE EVERY
EVENING SINCE
PARSIFAL VANISHED.

MY SON, Oh, THAT
THE COMING NIGHT
WOULD BRING YOU
TO YOUR MOTHER'S
ARMS AGAIN.
ROBBED OF SLEEP
AT NIGHT AND PEACE
BY DAY -- MY LOVER
DEAD, MY SON
STOLEN BY
SOME...

O,
dear
God.

SHE TREADS SLOWLY TO HER BED, SICK
WITH GRIEF, AND SUMMONS HER QUIET
STRENGTH TO A FINAL TEST.

DEAREST SAVIOR,
HEAR MY PRAYER.
LOOK NOT ON MY
ANGUISH, HEED NOT MY
TEARS, BUT HASTEN FROM
ME TO MY LOST SON
THAT HE MAY KNOW
YOUR BLESSING.

O LORD...

...SHALL HE
NEVER FEEL...

...A
DYING...

MOTHER'S
...

...KISS.

THE PAIN OF KNOWLEDGE WILL END IN REPENTANCE AND, WHEN YOU ARE ENLIGHTENED, THE IGNORANCE WHICH HAS TROUBLED YOUR HEART THESE MANY YEARS WILL VANISH. *PARSIFAL!* LEARN OF LIFE AND LOVE AS YOUR FATHER DID...

...WHEN *HERZELEIDE* FIRST SURRENDERED HER LIPS TO HIM. TAKE NOW, POOR CHILD, YOUR MOTHER'S LAST BLESSING AND THE FIRST KISS OF LOVE...

KUNDRY'S SEDUCTION IS COMPLETE -- BUT AS PARSIFAL RELEASES HIS GRIP ON THE MAGIC COIN HE HAS BEEN HOLDING, HIS MIND IS BATTERED WITH FRAGMENTS OF MEMORIES...

AMFORTAS!!

28

PARSIFAL
PART III: HIS VICTORY

AMFORTAS! *THE SOUND TEARS INTO HIS CONSCIOUSNESS. THE GLOWING OF THE GRAIL BLINDS HIS EYES AND HIS VERY SELF SPLITS IN TWO AS HE DOUBLES OVER IN PAIN...*

DEAR GOD! MY SIDE GAPES WITH A WOUND FROM THE HOLY SPEAR!

PARSIFAL STAGGERS UNDER A MASS OF MEMORIES, A PRECIPITOUS ONRUSH OF HITHERTO FORGOTTEN IDEAS, EVENTS, AND PEOPLE. AT LAST, AFTER ENDLESS YEARS OF SEARCHING AND IGNORANCE, **HE REMEMBERS:** *THE SECRETS OF HIS DEEP MIND ARE UNLOCKED BY THE KISS OF THIS WOMAN. AND HE FEELS THE SHARP STING OF A GASH IN HIS SIDE MADE BY COLD, ANCIENT METAL. PAIN CONTORTS HIS MIND AND BODY...*

WHA... WHAT AM I SAYING? I'M NOT BLEEDING!

BUT THE PAIN...

...THE SAME PAIN WHICH WRACKED AMFORTAS' MIGHTY FRAME WHEN HE, TOO, FELL PREY TO THE WITCH, KUNDRY, AND HER EVIL CHARMS. SLOWLY, PARSIFAL PENETRATES THE PARADOX...

HAVE I SO BETRAYED YOU, MY SAVIOR, THAT I MUST BEAR THIS DISGRACE?

IT IS THE VOICE OF AMFORTAS *IN ME!* IT IS *HIS* SUFFERING I FEEL--

ALSO CAUSED BY THE KISS OF *THIS WOMAN!*

KUNDRY LOOKS ON, ASTONISHED AT HEARING THE SAME WORDS SHE HAD HEARD BEFORE, SO LONG AGO.

WHY DOES HE SPEAK THE WORDS OF *AMFORTAS?*

AND WHY DID MY KISS NOT BRING HIM TO SUBMISSION?

NO ONE HAS EVER RESISTED ME!

HE HAS OVERCOME THE POWER OF THE CASTLED WIZARD WHO BINDS ME BY THE *CURSE* I BEAR!

COULD HE NOT *ALSO* OVERCOME THE POWER OF THE CURSE ITSELF!

OH, GOD!

WHY MUST I SEEK MY OWN DESTRUCTION WHEN I YEARN FOR *RELEASE?*

THE AGELESS SOUL IN THE TORTURED BODY OF KUNDRY FEELS PULLED APART BY HER DESIRES -- YET SHE PUTS NO REAL HOPE IN GOD'S SALVATION -- CENTURIES OF TORMENT CANNOT BE SHAKEN OFF SO EASILY -- BESIDES, SHE KNOWS THAT HER MASTER PARTICULARLY CRAVES THIS CAPTIVE FOR HIS CRUEL SPORTS.

PARSIFAL! YOU ARE BEWITCHED. LET ME...

NO, WOMAN!

I KNOW WHAT YOU *WANT* OF ME -- EVEN THOUGH I HAD NO KNOWLEDGE OF WHAT I WANTED *MYSELF* UNTIL YOUR KISS...

DARE YOU *TRUST* SUCH KNOWLEDGE, PARSIFAL?

MORE SURELY THAN I MAY TRUST *YOU!* AMFORTAS STILL LIES *WOUNDED* TRUSTING YOU!

HE EVEN SPEAKS AMFORTAS' *NAME!* CAN HE BE *BEYOND* KLINGSOR'S POWER?

I REMEMBER SEEING THE KING ONCE. *YES!* I WAS IN THE MOUNTAINS .....

"... AS I STOPPED BY A COLD LAKE TO WASH OFF THE WEARY MILES, TWO MAGNIFICENT SWANS ROSE UP AND CIRCLED IN THE BRIGHT BLUE SKY...

"I DREW MY BOW AND ONE OF THE BIRDS DROPPED LIKE A COMET AMID THE PINES...

"I RUSHED TO WHERE IT FELL AND BURST UPON AN OPEN GLADE FILLED WITH SOLEMN MEN SURROUNDING THE WHITE SWAN, ITS WINGS NOW MISSHAPEN AND LIMP, ITS FEATHERS SPATTERED WITH CRIMSON. I FOUND MYSELF AVOIDING THE PAIN-FILLED EYES OF THEIR COMMANDER WHO LAY ON HIS LITTER, HIS SIDE BOUND WITH ANOINTED CLOTH. YOUNG FOOL THAT I WAS, I STOOD IGNORANT AND ARROGANT BEFORE HIM -- THEN HE SPOKE OF THE NEEDLESS DEATH I HAD CAUSED -- AND OF MY GREAT NEED FOR REMORSE.

"I WAS RELUCTANTLY LED TO THE TEMPLE WHERE I SAW THE WOUNDED KING IN PRAYER BEFORE THE ALTER...

"I BEHELD THE GRAIL UNCOVERED -- THOUGH IT MEANT NOTHING TO ME AT THE TIME -- AS HE ADMINISTERED THE SACRAMENT. FIERCE, HOLY LIGHT SURROUNDED US, UNEARTHLY MUSIC FILLED THE HIGHEST DOME. AND THEN WITH A CRY HE *COLLAPSED*, THE WOUND IN HIS SIDE SPLITTING OPEN. I WAS TOLD THIS HAPPENED WHENEVER DUTY DEMANDED THAT AMFORTAS FULFILL HIS PRIESTLY OFFICE...

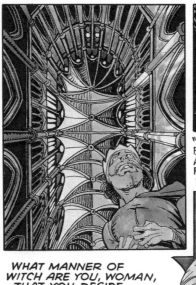

"...JUST AS IT HAD DONE WHEN *YOU* BETRAYED HIM WITH YOUR KISSES -- AND THE HOLY SPEAR WAS STOLEN FROM HIM AND RIPPED INTO HIS SAINTLY BODY.

WHAT MANNER OF WITCH ARE YOU, WOMAN, THAT YOU DESIRE THE DESTRUCTION OF ALL THAT IS SACRED?

31

KUNDRY HESITATES -- CAN SHE **TELL** HIM THE TRUTH? AND WILL THIS IMPETUOUS BOY BE ABLE TO **BREAK** THE SPELL WHICH BINDS HER TO KLINGSOR, WHO EVEN NOW IS SPEAKING TO HER INNER MIND, DEMANDING THAT SHE MUST OBEY...

MY KISS HAS EXPOSED THE DEEP SECRETS OF YOUR FORGOTTEN PAST TO YOU. I HAVE RESTORED TO YOU YOUR IDENTITY -- AND *STILL* YOU WOULD DEFAME ME!

PARSIFAL! I HAVE TAUGHT YOU NOTHING IF YOU HAVE NOT LEARNED PITY!

FOR TIME BEYOND RECALL I HAVE WANDERED THIS EARTH... TIME THAT HAS WORN MY MIND UNTIL LITTLE THAT IS A WOMAN'S BY RIGHT IS LEFT TO ME!

I BEAR A BURDEN FAR GREATER THAN THE LOAD OF IGNORANCE OF WHICH I HAVE RELIEVED YOU... YOU SEE...

I SAW HIM!

HIM, PARSIFAL!

I SAW THE MAN STAGGER UNDER THE INHUMAN YOKE OF SIN AND IGNORANCE BY WHICH HE WAS TO DIE, THOUGH INNOCENT.

I SAW THE PLAITED, THORNED CROWN PIERCE HIS FOREHEAD, DRIPPING BLOOD IN HIS EYES...

...AS *I* LAY IN THE ARMS OF A RICH ROMAN ON HIS PORCH THAT DARK MORNING IN JERUSALEM. I THOUGHT THIS MAN WITH BLEEDING FEET AND WOEFUL EYES TO BE A *FOOL* --

AND AS HE PASSED...

I LAUGHED AT HIM!

HAHAHAHA HAHAHA HAHA

I HAVE PASSED THROUGH MANY LIFETIMES SINCE THEN, WANDERING ENDLESS. I HAVE PRAYED FOR DEATH, BUT IT HAS BEEN DENIED ME BY THE CURSE WHICH I BROUGHT UPON MYSELF...

I HAVE ONLY THIS LIVING DEATH IN WHICH I LAUGH AT THE DEPLORABLE AND DESPERATE...

I HAVE STRETCHED OUT MY ARMS TO THOSE WHO SOUGHT A HOLY LIFE...

...ONLY TO ENTICE THEM TO LUST AND RENUNCIATION OF THEIR FAITH.

MANY HAVE JOINED THE LEGIONS OF THE DAMNED THROUGH ME.

I HAVE BEEN A READY TOOL IN THE HANDS OF MAGICIANS WHO...

BUT KUNDRY'S TONGUE IS STAYED-- HER MASTER FEARS FOR HIS PLAN...

HIS POWER EXTENDS ONLY OVER THOSE WHO HAVE *FALLEN*-- AND IF THIS BOY IS TO BE USED AS A STEPPING STONE TO EVENTUAL CONTROL OF THE GRAIL HE MUST BE *INDUCED* INTO RELINQUISHING HIS PRECIOUS PURITY. KUNDRY FEELS HERSELF BEING PULLED APART BY KLINGSOR'S CONTROL AND HER OWN OPPOSING DESIRE FOR SALVATION... BUT HER TASK IS *SET*...

WHAT CAN I DO FOR YOU, WOMAN, BUT TO ENJOIN YOU TO *KNEEL* WITH ME IN PRAYER AND REPENTANCE?

OH, CHILD! DO YOU NOT THINK THAT MY VOICE IS *HOARSE* WITH SUPPLICATIONS TO A GOD WHOM I NOW CAN ONLY MOCK?

IF YOU DESIRE ANY PEACE FOR MY SOUL, DEAL MERCIFULLY WITH ME. YOU ALONE KNOW MY TORMENTED PAST-- I FEEL STRANGELY CONTENTED IN YOUR PRESENCE...

...FOR YOU, TOO, HAVE SUFFERED SO UNJUSTLY.

PARSIFAL! IF YOU WOULD STAY WITH ME BUT ONE NIGHT AND HOLD ME IN YOUR ARMS AS YOUR OWN...

... I *KNOW* THAT THE FEVER WHICH HAS BURNED IN MY BODY FOR SO LONG WOULD BE EXTINGUISHED IN A FLAME OF DESIRE-- A DESIRE TO SATISFY YOU ALONE...

STOP, WITCH! THE STENCH OF BRIMSTONE AL-READY BURNS MY NOSTRILS AS YOU BREATHE YOUR INVITATION TO THE DANCE DEATH! DO YOU NOT RECOGNIZE THAT YOUR DELIVERANCE IS AT HAND?

35

DEATH SLICES THE AIR BEFORE HIM, BUT WITH FAITH IN GOD'S LOVE, PARSIFAL SEES THE FATAL COURSE OF THE SPEAR **TURN** SO THAT IT COMES TO REST ABOVE HIS HEAD, HOVERING IN A HOLY LIGHT...

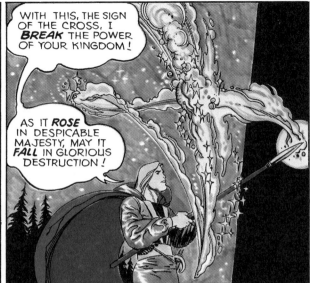

WITH THIS, THE SIGN OF THE CROSS, I **BREAK** THE POWER OF YOUR KINGDOM!

AS IT **ROSE** IN DESPICABLE MAJESTY, MAY IT **FALL** IN GLORIOUS DESTRUCTION!

A SPEECHLESS TERROR SEIZES KLINGSOR AS HE FEELS THE WALLS AROUND HIM MOVING WITHIN THEMSELVES. THE SPELLS WHICH ERECTED HIS FORTRESS ARE RETURNING TO THEIR SOURCE...

A VACUUM PULLS THE ELEMENTS INTO WHIRLWIND. THE TWO IN THE GARDEN BELOW LOOK ON -- ONE IN RAPTURE... THE OTHER AGHAST...

THE EARTH ROCKS IN ITS TIMELESS PATH AS THE EVIL INTENT OF CENTURIES OF BLACK MAGIC DRAWS TOGETHER IN A DEAFENING AND HORRIFIC

IMPLOSION
OF ITSELF...

...AND ALL THE ASPIRATIONS OF A FEEBLE MAN LAY CRUMPLED AMONG THE ROCKS AND RUIN.

THE QUILT ACKNOWLEDGMENT OF SUNRISE GREETS THE BOY-TURNED-MAN. WHERE THE ILLUSION OF FOREST AND GARDEN WAS, HE NOW SEES ONLY THE DESERT-- BARREN, BUT REAL. THE WRETCHED KUNDRY FEARS TO MOVE...

KUNDRY, YOU DEAR, DESPERATE WOMAN, YOU HAVE CURSED ME TO NEVER FIND THE PATH WHICH LEADS TO AMFORTAS --

--YET, IT IS *THERE* WE SHALL MEET AGAIN...

WANDERING, NEVER TO FIND THE PATH HE SEEKS, PARSIFAL'S HEART IS NEVERTHELESS NOW FILLED WITH THE LIFE-GIVING STRENGTH OF GOD -- AND HIS HAND BEARS EASILY THE WEIGHT OF THE SPEAR WHICH WILL SOMEDAY HEAL THE KING. *PARSIFAL'S* WAY IS PREPARED...

...AND *KUNDRY*, IN SPITE OF HER OWN CURSE, YET SEES ON THE HORIZON A JOY BEYOND HER BITTER LAUGHTER, GRACE BEYOND HER MOST EVIL DEED...

39

FOR OUR FRIEND AND TEACHER — JUDY MOORE

Salomé

INTRODUCTION

Oscar Wilde's play *Salomé* and Richard Strauss's operatic adaptation have long had a reputation of 'shocking depravity'. In its early years the opera was banned on numerous occasions. Frau Wittich, the dramatic soprano, who was the first Salomé, protested in rehearsal, 'I won't do it. I'm a decent woman.' The character of Salomé is, in fact, one of the great moral figures in all opera. Even John the Baptist (as conceived by Wilde) in his blind rigidity, his total lack of compassion, pales in contrast to the sixteen-year-old oriental princess. Raised in the most decadent of worlds, the virgin princess has retained her purity for sixteen years. She worships the chaste goddess of the moon and has remained untouched by the all-encompassing corruption of Herod's court. Salomé's first awareness of John the Baptist is that of a voice prophesying a great retribution, a cleansing of filth and corruption. It is her first encounter with a firmly held ethical standard. To Salomé, his voice, like the voice of God, is like a light in the wilderness. It is significant that Salomé hears John before she sees him. Her attraction then is not primarily physical, but spiritual (ethical) and, upon his emergence from the cistern, is made whole by physical attraction. Salomé is ready to give her virginity to the highest standard of virtue she has witnessed. Her mind-body integrity is complete.

The play's central conflict arises when Salomé, whose spiritual yearnings are expressed through her physical self, approaches the man to whom only the non-physical is sacred.

And it is from there that the conflict intensifies in Salomé's mind, leading the story to its tragic conclusion.

P. Craig Russell

Salomé by Oscar Wilde

Adapted for Comics by P. Craig Russell — •OP. 23•

Lettering by Ken Bruzenak

43

44

AFTER ME SHALL COME ANOTHER MIGHTIER THAN I. I AM NOT WORTHY SO MUCH AS TO UNLOOSE THE LATCHET OF HIS SHOES. WHEN HE COMETH, THE SOLITARY PLACES SHALL BE GLAD. WHEN HE COMETH, THE EYES OF THE BLIND SHALL SEE THE DAY, AND THE EARS OF THE DEAF SHALL BE OPENED.

MAKE HIM BE SILENT.

HE IS A HOLY MAN.

HE IS ALWAYS SAYING RIDICULOUS THINGS.

HE IS VERY GENTLE, EVERY DAY, WHEN I GIVE HIM TO EAT HE THANKS ME.

WHO IS HE?

WHAT IS HIS NAME?

A PROPHET.

JOKANAAN.

WHENCE COMES HE?

FROM THE DESERT. A GREAT MULTITUDE USED TO FOLLOW HIM.

IT IS IMPOSSIBLE TO UNDERSTAND WHAT HE SAYS.

WHAT IS HE TALKING OF?

MAY ONE SEE HIM?

NO!

THE TETRARCH HAS FORBIDDEN IT.

WHAT A STRANGE PRISON--AN OLD CISTERN. THAT MUST BE A POISONOUS PLACE IN WHICH TO DWELL.

OH, NO! FOR INSTANCE, THE TETRARCH'S BROTHER, HIS ELDER BROTHER, THE FIRST HUSBAND OF HERODIAS THE QUEEN, WAS IMPRISONED HERE FOR TWELVE YEARS. IT DID NOT KILL HIM. AT THE END OF TWELVE YEARS HE HAD TO BE STRANGLED.

45

YES, SHE IS COMING TOWARDS US.

I PRAY YOU NOT TO LOOK AT HER.

SHE IS LIKE A NARCISSUS TREMBLING IN THE WIND...

...SHE IS LIKE A SILVER FLOWER...

...SHE IS LIKE A DOVE THAT HAS STRAYED.

I WILL NOT STAY, *I CANNOT STAY!* WHY DOES THE TETRARCH LOOK AT ME ALL THE WHILE WITH HIS MOLE'S EYES UNDER HIS SHAKING EYELIDS? IT IS STRANGE THAT THE HUSBAND OF MY MOTHER LOOKS AT ME LIKE THAT. I KNOW NOT WHAT IT MEANS.

OF A TRUTH, I KNOW IT TOO WELL.

HOW SWEET THE AIR IS HERE! I CAN BREATHE HERE!

WITHIN, THERE ARE JEWS FROM JERUSALEM WHO ARE TEARING EACH OTHER IN PIECES OVER THEIR FOOLISH CEREMONIES...

THERE ARE BARBARIANS WHO DRINK AND DRINK AND SPILL THEIR WINE ON THE PAVEMENT, AND GREEKS FROM SMYRNA WITH PAINTED EYES AND PAINTED CHEEKS, AND EGYPTIANS SILENT AND SUBTLE WITH LONG PAINTED NAILS OF JADE, AND BRUTAL, COARSE ROMANS...

...AH! HOW I *LOATHE* THE ROMANS!

SOMETHING TERRIBLE WILL HAPPEN. WHY DO YOU LOOK AT HER?

47

REJOICE NOT, O LAND OF PALESTINE, BECAUSE THE ROD OF HIM WHO SMOTE THEE IS BROKEN. FOR FROM THE SEED OF THE SERPENT SHALL COME A BASILISK, AND THAT WHICH IS BORN OF IT SHALL DEVOUR THE BIRDS!

WHAT A STRANGE VOICE! I WOULD SPEAK WITH HIM!

THE TETRARCH DOES NOT SUFFER ANYONE TO SPEAK WITH HIM, PRINCESS. HE HAS EVEN FORBIDDEN THE HIGH PRIEST TO SPEAK WITH HIM.

I WILL SPEAK WITH HIM.

WE DARE NOT, PRINCESS.

HOW BLACK IT IS DOWN THERE.

IT MUST BE TERRIBLE TO BE IN SO BLACK A HOLE!

IT IS LIKE A TOMB...

DID YOU NOT HEAR ME? BRING OUT THE PROPHET. I WOULD LOOK ON HIM.

BUT THE TETRARCH HAS FORMALLY FORBIDDEN THAT ANY MAN SHOULD RAISE THE COVER OF THIS WELL.

THOU WILT DO THIS THING FOR ME, NARRABOTH, AND TOMORROW WHEN I PASS IN MY LITTER BENEATH THE GATE-WAY OF THE IDOL-SELLERS, I WILL LET FALL FOR THEE A LITTLE FLOWER, A LITTLE GREEN FLOWER.

PRINCESS, I CANNOT, I CANNOT!

THOU WILT DO THIS THING FOR ME, NARRABOTH. THOU KNOWEST THAT THOU WILT DO THIS THING FOR ME, AND ON THE MORROW, WHEN I SHALL PASS IN MY LITTER BY THE BRIDGE OF THE IDOL-BUYERS, I WILL LOOK AT THEE THROUGH THE MUSLIN VEILS. IT MAY BE I WILL SMILE AT THEE. LOOK AT ME, NARRABOTH, LOOK AT ME. AH, THOU KNOWEST THOU WILT DO WHAT I ASK THEE... THOU KNOWEST IT.

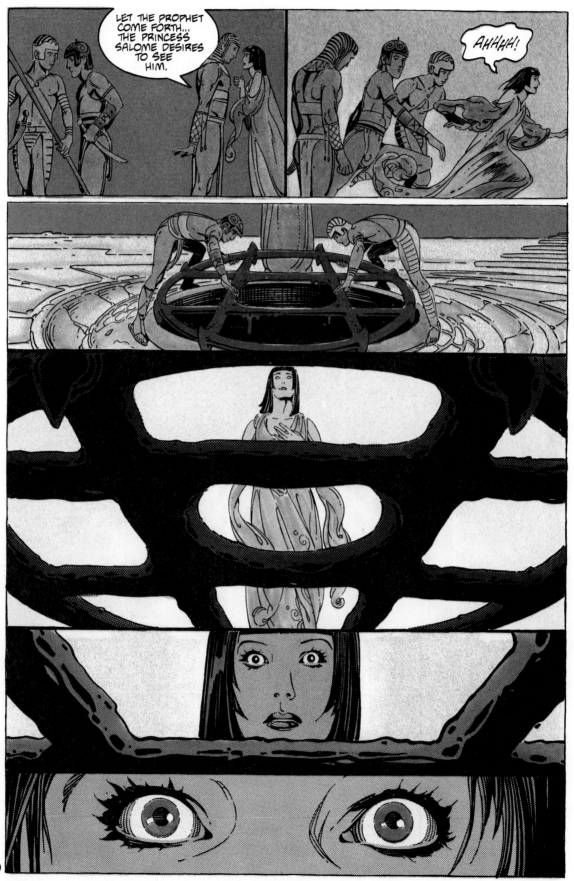

WHERE IS HE WHOSE CUP OF ABOMINATION IS NOW FULL? WHERE IS HE, WHO, IN A ROBE OF SILVER, SHALL ONE DAY DIE IN THE FACE OF ALL THE PEOPLE? BID HIM COME FORTH, THAT HE MAY HEAR THE VOICE OF HIM WHO CRIED IN THE WASTE PLACES AND IN THE HOUSES OF KINGS!

OF WHOM IS HE SPEAKING?

NO ONE CAN TELL, PRINCESS.

WHERE IS SHE WHO SAW THE IMAGES OF MEN PAINTED ON THE WALLS, EVEN OF THE IMAGES OF THE CHALDEANS PAINTED WITH COLORS, AND GAVE HERSELF UP TO LUST OF HER EYES, AND SENT AMBASSADORS TO THE LAND OF CHALDEA?

IT IS OF MY MOTHER HE IS SPEAKING.

OH, NO, PRINCESS!

YES, IT IS OF MY MOTHER.

WHERE IS SHE WHO GAVE HERSELF UNTO THE CAPTAINS OF ASSYRIA? WHERE IS SHE WHO HATH GIVEN HERSELF TO THE YOUNG MEN OF THE EGYPTIANS, WHOSE SHIELDS ARE OF GOLD, WHOSE HELMETS ARE OF SILVER, WHOSE BODIES ARE MIGHTY? GO, BID HER RISE UP FROM THE BED OF HER INCESTUOUSNESS, THAT SHE MAY HEAR THE WORDS OF HIM WHO PREPARETH THE WAY OF THE LORD, THAT SHE MAY REPENT HER OF HER INIQUITIES. THOUGH SHE WILL NOT REPENT; GO, BID HER COME, FOR THE ROD OF THE LORD IS IN HIS HAND.

51

52

WHO IS HE, THE SON OF MAN? IS HE AS BEAUTIFUL AS THOU?

GET THEE BEHIND ME! I HEAR IN THE PALACE THE BEATING OF THE WINGS OF THE ANGEL OF DEATH.

...JOKANAAN!

PRINCESS...

I AM AMOROUS OF THY BODY, JOKANAAN! THY BODY IS WHITE LIKE THE SNOWS THAT LIE ON THE MOUNTAINS OF JUDEA, NEITHER THE ROSES IN THE GARDEN OF THE QUEEN OF ARABIA, NOR THE FEET OF OF THE DAWN WHEN THEY LIGHT ON THE LEAVES, NOR THE BREAST OF THE MOON WHEN SHE LIES ON THE BREAST OF THE SEA... THERE IS NOTHING IN THE WORLD SO WHITE AS THY BODY...

LET ME TOUCH THY BODY.

BACK, DAUGHTER OF BABYLON! I WILL NOT LISTEN TO THEE. I LISTEN BUT TO THE VOICE OF THE LORD GOD.

THY BODY IS HIDEOUS! IT IS LIKE THE BODY OF A LEPER. IT IS LIKE A PLASTERED WALL, WHERE THE SCORPIONS HAVE MADE THEIR NEST. IT IS HORRIBLE, THY BODY IS HORRIBLE.

IT IS THY HAIR THAT I AM ENAMOURED OF, JOKANAAN. THY HAIR IS LIKE THE CLUSTERS OF BLACK GRAPES THAT HANG FROM THE VINE-TREES OF EDOM. THY HAIR IS LIKE THE CEDARS OF LEBANON THAT GIVE THEIR SHADE TO THE LIONS AND TO THE ROBBERS, THE LONG BLACK NIGHTS, WHEN THE MOON HIDES HER FACE, WHEN THE STARS ARE AFRAID, ARE NOT SO BLACK AS THY HAIR...

LET ME TOUCH THY HAIR.

DAUGHTER OF SODOM, TOUCH ME NOT. PROFANE NOT THE TEMPLE OF THE LORD GOD.

THY HAIR IS HORRIBLE! IT IS COVERED WITH MIRE AND DUST. IT IS LIKE A KNOT OF SERPENTS COILED ROUND THY NECK.

I LOVE NOT THY HAIR...

IT IS THY MOUTH THAT I DESIRE, JOKANAAN.

53

THY MOUTH IS LIKE A POMEGRANITE CUT WITH A KNIFE OF IVORY. THE RED BLASTS OF TRUMPETS THAT HERALD THE APPROACH OF KINGS, AND MAKE AFRAID THE ENEMY, ARE NOT SO RED.

THY MOUTH IS REDDER THAN THE FEET OF THOSE WHO TREAD THE WINE IN THE WINE-PRESS, IT IS REDDER THAN THE FEET OF THE DOVES WHO HAUNT THE TEMPLES, THERE IS NOTHING IN THE WORLD SO RED AS THY MOUTH...

LET ME KISS THY MOUTH.

NEVER! DAUGHTER OF BABYLON, DAUGHTER OF SODOM... NEVER.

PRINCESS, *PRINCESS*, THOU WHO ART THE DOVE OF ALL DOVES, LOOK NOT AT THIS MAN, LOOK NOT AT HIM! DO NOT SPEAK SUCH WORDS TO HIM. I CANNOT ENDURE IT...

I WILL KISS THY MOUTH, JOKANAAN.

LET ME KISS THY MOUTH.

DAUGHTER OF ADULTERY, THERE IS BUT ONE WHO CAN SAVE THEE; IT IS HE OF WHOM I SPAKE. GO SEEK HIM. HE IS ON A BOAT IN THE SEA OF GALILEE, AND HE TALKETH WITH HIS DISCIPLES. KNEEL DOWN ON THE SHORE OF THE SEA, AND CALL UPON HIM BY HIS NAME. WHEN HE COMETH TO THEE (AND TO ALL WHO CALL ON HIM HE COMETH), BOW THYSELF AT HIS FEET AND ASK HIM THE REMISSIONS OF THY SINS.

LET ME KISS THY MOUTH.

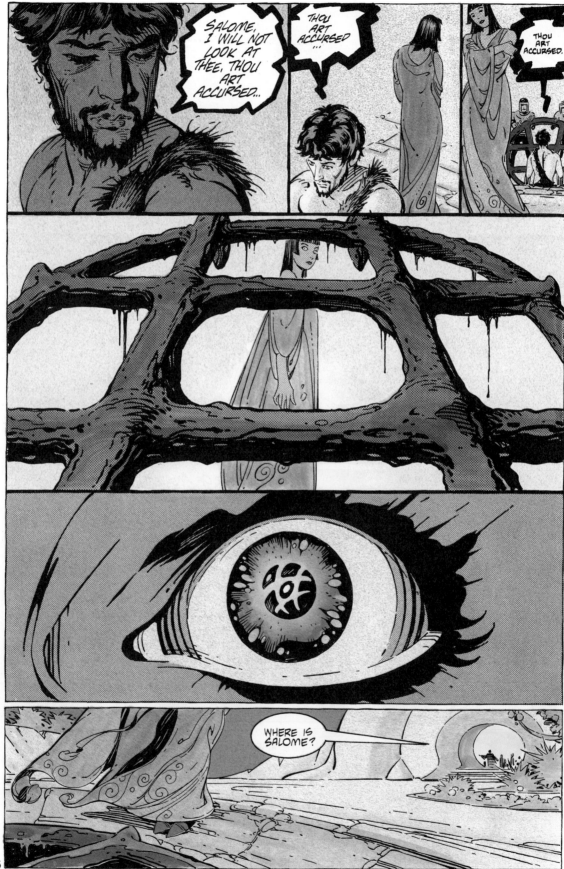

59

61

62

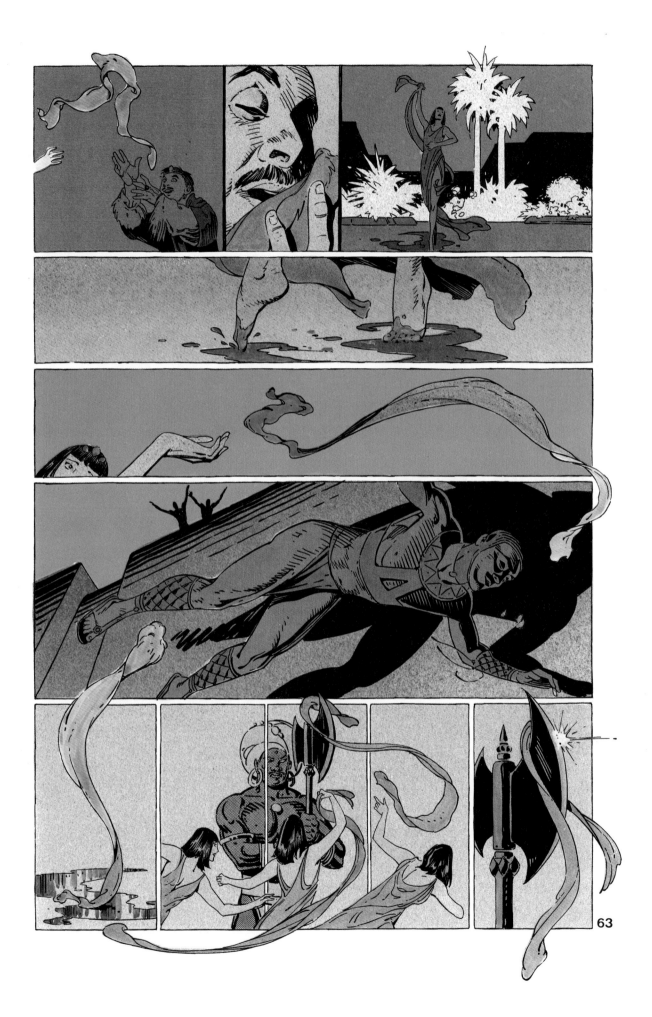

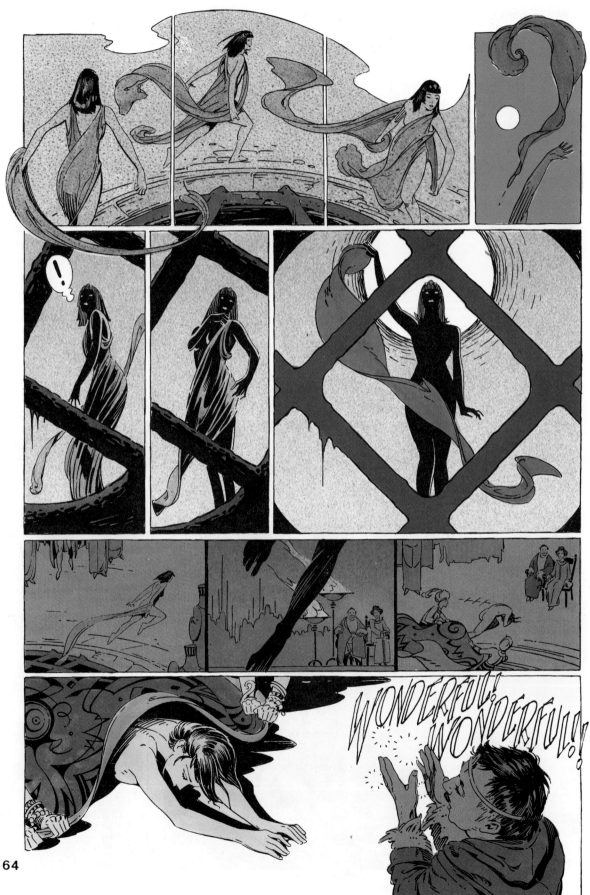

64

YOU SEE THAT SHE HAS DANCED FOR ME, YOUR DAUGHTER.

COME NEAR, SALOME. I WILL GIVE THEE WHATSOEVER THY SOUL DESIRETH. WHAT WOULDST THOU HAVE?

SPEAK!

I WOULD THAT THEY PRESENTLY BRING ME, IN A SILVER CHARGER ...

IN A SILVER CHARGER? SURELY, YES, IN A SILVER CHARGER. SHE IS CHARMING, IS SHE NOT?

WHAT WOULD YOU HAVE THEM BRING THEE IN A SILVER CHARGER?

THE HEAD OF JOKANAAN!

OH, NO...

AH!!! THAT IS WELL SAID, MY DAUGHTER!

MY DAUGHTER HAS DONE WELL TO ASK THE HEAD OF JOKANAAN. HE HAS COVERED ME WITH INSULTS. ONE CAN SEE THAT SHE LOVES HER MOTHER WELL. DO NOT YIELD, MY DAUGHTER. HE HAS SWORN.

PEACE!

SALOME, I PRAY THEE, BE REASONABLE. THE HEAD OF A MAN THAT IS CUT FROM HIS BODY IS ILL TO LOOK UPON. HEARKEN TO ME. I HAVE AN EMERALD, A GREAT EMERALD. IT IS THE LARGEST EMERALD IN THE WHOLE WORLD. ASK IT OF ME AND I WILL GIVE IT THEE.

THE HEAD OF JOKANAAN.

YOU SAY THAT TO TROUBLE ME, BECAUSE I HAVE LOOKED AT YOU ALL THIS EVENING. YOUR BEAUTY TROUBLED ME. SALOME, YOU KNOW MY WHITE PEACOCKS, MY BEAUTIFUL WHITE PEACOCKS? THERE IS NO KING IN ALL THE WORLD WHO POSSESSES SUCH PEACOCKS. I HAVE BUT A HUNDRED. BUT I WILL GIVE THEM ALL TO YOU

THE HEAD OF JOKANAAN.

WELL SAID, MY DAUGHTER! AS FOR YOU, YOU ARE RIDICULOUS WITH YOUR PEACOCKS!

BE SILENT! SALOME, THINK OF WHAT YOU ARE DOING. HE IS A HOLY MAN.

THE HEAD OF JOKANAAN.

AH! YOU ARE NOT LISTENING TO ME. BE CALM, SALOME. I AM QUITE CALM.

LISTEN. I HAVE JEWELS HIDDEN IN THIS PLACE-- JEWELS THAT YOUR MOTHER EVEN HAS NEVER SEEN. I WILL GIVE THEM ALL TO YOU.

I HAVE TOPAZES, AS YELLOW AS THE EYES OF TIGERS, OPALS THAT BURN ALWAYS, AND ONYXES LIKE THE EYEBALLS OF A DEAD WOMAN...

I HAVE CRYSOLITES AND BERYLS AND SARDONYX... THE KING OF THE INDIES HAS SENT ME FOUR FANS OF PARROT FEATHERS, AND THE KING OF NUMIDIA A GARMENT OF OSTRICH PLUME...

I HAVE A CRYSTAL INTO WHICH IT IS NOT LAWFUL FOR A WOMAN TO LOOK, NOR MAY YOUNG MEN BEHOLD UNTIL THEY HAVE BEEN BEATEN WITH RODS...THREE TORQUOISES, HE WHO WEARS THEM CAN IMAGINE THINGS WHICH ARE NOT...

THEY ARE TREASURES WITHOUT PRICE. WHAT DESIREST THOU MORE THAN THIS, SALOME? I WILL GIVE THEE ALL THAT IS MINE, SAVE ONE LIFE. I WILL GIVE THEE THE MANTLE OF THE HIGH PRIEST...

I WILL GIVE THEE THE VEIL OF THE SANCTUARY.

!עעעעעעם

GIVE ME THE HEAD OF JOKANAAN.

LET HER BE GIVEN WHAT SHE ASKS. OF A TRUTH, SHE IS HER MOTHER'S CHILD.

66

...BUT, WHEREFORE, DOST THOU NOT LOOK AT ME, JOKANAAN? THINE EYES THAT WERE SO TERRIBLE, SO FULL OF RAGE AND SCORN, ARE SHUT NOW. ART THOU AFRAID OF ME, JOKANAAN, THAT THOU WILT NOT LOOK AT ME?

...AND THY TONGUE, IT SAYS NOTHING NOW, JOKANAAN, THAT SCARLET VIPER THAT SPAT ITS VENOM UPON ME. HOW IS IT THAT THE RED VIPER STIRS NO LONGER?

THOU DIDST SPEAK EVIL WORDS AGAINST *ME*, *ME*, SALOME, DAUGHTER OF HERODIAS, PRINCESS OF JUDEA.

WELL, JOKANAAN, I STILL LIVE, BUT THOU, *THOU* ART DEAD, AND THY HEAD BELONGS TO ME.

I CAN DO WITH IT WHAT I WILL.

I CAN THROW IT TO THE DOGS AND TO THE BIRDS OF THE AIR. THAT WHICH *THE DOGS LEAVE, THE BIRDS OF THE AIR SHALL DEVOUR*....

AH! JOKANAAN, JOKANAAN, THOU WERT BEAUTIFUL.

69

THY BODY WAS A COLUMN OF IVORY SET ON A SILVER SOCKET. IT WAS A GARDEN FULL OF DOVES AND OF SILVER LILIES. THERE WAS NOTHING IN THE WORLD SO WHITE AS THY BODY.

THERE WAS NOTHING IN THE WORLD SO BLACK AS THY HAIR. THE SILENCE THAT DWELLS IN THE FOREST WAS NOT SO BLACK.

IN THE WHOLE WORLD THERE WAS NOTHING SO RED AS THY MOUTH. THY VOICE WAS A CENSER. AND WHEN I LOOKED ON THEE I HEARD A STRANGE MUSIC.

AH! WHEREFORE DIDST THOU NOT LOOK AT ME, JOKANAAN?

THOU DIDST PUT UPON THINE EYES THE COVERING OF HIM WHO WOULD SEE HIS GOD.

WELL, THOU HAST SEEN THY GOD, JOKANAAN, BUT ME, ME, ME, THOU DIDST NEVER SEE.

IF THOU HADST SEEN ME THOU WOULDST HAVE LOVED ME.

72

73

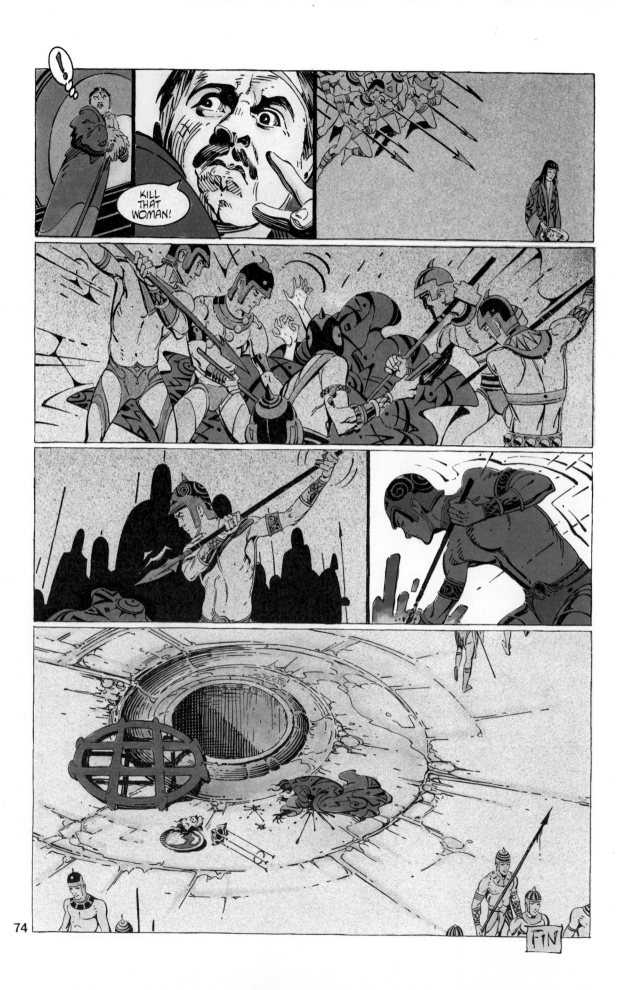

74

MAHLER

INTRODUCTION

Austrian composer Gustav Mahler (1860-1911) brought the orchestral song to new heights. His work represents an almost perfect synthesis of the Romantic interests in folk song, tradition, and nationalism.

Both *Unto this World* (from *Fünf Lieder nach Rückert*, 1901-4), and *The Drinking Song of Earth's Sorrow* (from *Lied von der Erde*, 1908), are fine examples of his intimate songs for vocalist and small orchestra.

Letitia Glozer

The Drinking Song of Earth's Sorrow

TRANSLATED FROM THE GERMAN BY PATRICK C. MASON

PCR #16

THOUGH THE WINE BECKONS FROM ITS GOLDEN CHALICE...DO NOT DRINK YET! FIRST HEAR MY SONG

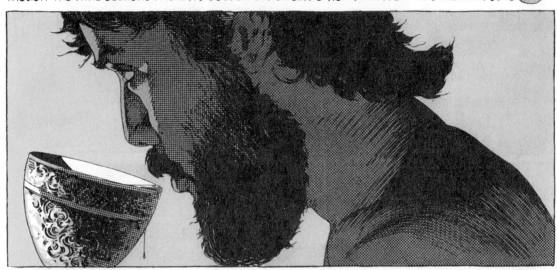

A SONG OF SORROW, FULL OF BITTER LAUGHTER CLANGING THROUGH THE SOUL.

FOR WHEN GRIEF APPROACHES IT DESTROYS THE SOUL'S FAIR GARDENS.

JOY AND SINGING DIE OFF INTO WHIMPERS

DARK IS LIFE
DARK IS DEATH

77

MASTER OF THE HOUSE! YOU HAVE A CELLAR
LAID HEAVY WITH THE BEST WINE.

AND I HAVE HERE A LUTE OF MY
OWN.

TO STRIKE THE LUTE,
AND EMPTY THE GLASS--
THESE THINGS ARE WELL WED.

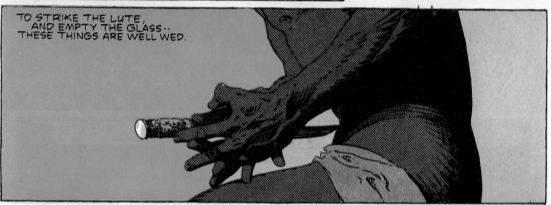

A CUP OF WINE
AT THE RIGHT
MOMENT--

--IS OF FAR GREATER
VALUE THAN ALL
THIS WORLD
HAS TO OFFER.

DARK IS LIFE
DARK IS DEATH

THE SKY REMAINS
FOREVER BLUE
AND THE FAITHFUL OLD
EARTH BLOOMS EVERY
SPRING.
BUT YOU--O MAN--
HOW LONG WILL YOU
REMAIN?

NOT YET ONE HUNDRED YEARS IS GIVEN YOU TO ENJOY THE PUTRID FRUIT OF THIS SOIL.

LOOK! DOWN THERE IN THE MOONLIGHT, A WILD SPECTRAL SHAPE SQUATS AMONG THE GRAVES.

IT'S AN APE! HEAR HOW ITS HOWLING POLLUTES THE SWEET AIR OF THIS LIFE.

NOW--TAKE UP THE WINE! NOW--NOW THE TIME IS RIGHT, MY FRIENDS!

DRAIN YOUR GOLDEN CHALICES TO THE DREGS.

79

DARK IS LIFE DARK IS DEATH

UNTO THIS WORLD

I AM BECOME LOST
TO THE WORLD,
WITH WHOM I WASTED SO
MUCH TIME.

SHE HAS HEARD NOTHING
OF ME FOR SO LONG,

-SHE MAY WELL BELIEVE THAT I AM DEAD.

IT IS OF NO
CONCERN TO
ME AT ALL
THAT SHE
THINKS ME
DEAD —

HOW CAN I
POSSIBLY
REFUTE
HER?

FOR, TRULY,
I AM
DEAD—

—DEAD TO THE
WORLD.

I AM DEAD TO THIS
RAVING WORLD—

—AND AT REST IN THE
STILLNESS OF
SERENITY.

I LIVE ALONE IN MY HEAVEN,

IN MY LOVES,

-IN MY SONG

82

FIN

PELLÉAS & MELISANDE

INTRODUCTION

'A new indescribable power dominates this somnambulistic drama. All that is said therein at once hides and reveals the source of an unknown life.' So did Maurice Maeterlinck write of Ibsen's play *The Master Builder*, but the observation is remarkably true of his own work, which 'at once hides and reveals' its symbols, ideas, and characters.

Maurice Polydore-Marie-Bernard Maeterlinck was born in Ghent in 1862 and, though the greatest of all Belgian playwrights, he wrote in French. Indeed, his strongest influences were from the French Symbolist poets and his expression of the ideas of the Symbolists in drama is his great achievement. Though much admired in his own day for his poetry and philosophical prose as well as his many and varied works for the stage, it is a single play, *Pelléas and Melisande* (1892) by which he is known today. It is the undisputed masterpiece of both the author and the era.

Maeterlinck embodied some striking contradictions. A mystic who was involved in the occult in his early years, he was also an avid bicyclist and health enthusiast. (He died in 1949 at the age of 86). His philosophical pessimism is strangely offset by the constant suggestion throughout his work that man just may be able to understand himself and by such an appreciation even effect a change for the better in the human condition. But there is no clear ideology or plan set forth in his work — only speculation.

The Symbolists and especially Maeterlinck felt that the spoken word was somewhat impotent. Perhaps that is why *Pelléas and Melisande* is known primarily through Claude Debussy's sensitive musical setting. But if something is lacking in the words of this dream-play, it is only because something is lacking in language for Maeterlinck. The music of Debussy or the artwork of Russell may enunciate the action and meanings of the drama, but it remains a world of half-lives, ephemeral yet recognizable in some distracted corner of our minds.

Parick C. Mason

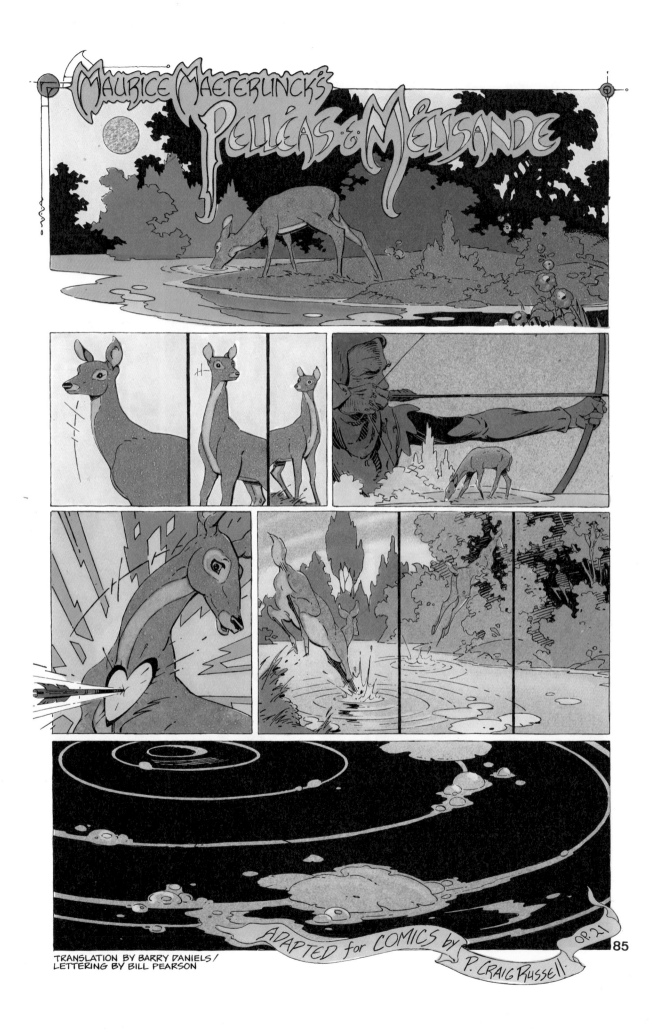

MAURICE MAETERLINCK'S
PELLÉAS & MÉLISANDE

ADAPTED for COMICS by
P. CRAIG RUSSELL

OP. 21

85

TRANSLATION BY BARRY DANIELS /
LETTERING BY BILL PEARSON

A GIRL AT THE WATER'S EDGE, WEEPING! SHE DOESN'T HEAR ME. I CAN'T SEE HER FACE.

WHY ARE YOU WEEPING? DON'T BE AFRAID. YOU HAVE NOTHING TO FEAR... WHY ARE YOU HERE ALL ALONE, WEEPING?

DON'T TOUCH ME! DON'T TOUCH ME!

DON'T BE AFRAID... I WILL NOT DO YOU...

...ANY—

OH! YOU ARE LOVELY!

88

89

②

HERE IS WHAT HE WRITES HIS BROTHER PELLEAS:

"ONE NIGHT, LOST IN THE FOREST, I FOUND HER WEEPING ON THE SHORE OF A LAKE. I DON'T KNOW HER AGE, NOR WHO SHE IS, NOR WHERE SHE IS FROM. I CANNOT QUESTION HER -- SHE MUST HAVE HAD A GREAT SHOCK, AND WHEN SHE IS ASKED WHAT HAPPENED, SHE BURSTS INTO TEARS LIKE A CHILD. HER SOBS FILL ME WITH TERROR! WE HAVE BEEN MARRIED SIX MONTHS NOW, AND I KNOW NO MORE THAN ON THE DAY OF OUR MEETING. IN THE MEANTIME, DEAR PELLEAS, WHOM I LOVE MORE THAN A BROTHER ALTHOUGH WE ARE NOT SONS OF THE SAME FATHER, GET READY FOR MY RETURN. -- I KNOW THAT MY MOTHER WILL GLADLY FORGIVE ME. BUT I FEAR ARKEL, IN SPITE OF ALL HIS GOODNESS. WITH THIS STRANGE MARRIAGE, I HAVE UPSET HIS POLITICAL MANEUVERS. IF, NEVERTHELESS, HE CONSENTS TO WELCOME HER, ON THE THIRD DAY AFTER THIS LETTER ARRIVES, LIGHT A LAMP AT THE TOP OF THE TOWER OVERLOOKING THE SEA. I WILL SEE IT FROM OUR SHIP -- IF NOT, I WILL GO AWAY, NEVER TO COME BACK...."

WHAT DO YOU SAY TO THAT?

I'VE NOTHING TO SAY...

UNTIL TODAY, HE HAD ALWAYS FOLLOWED MY ADVICE -- I HAD HOPED FOR HIS HAPPINESS, SENDING HIM TO ASK FOR THE HAND OF PRINCESS URSULA...

HE COULD NOT CONTINUE ALONE. SINCE HIS WIFE'S DEATH, HE HAS BEEN SAD, LIVING ALONE.

AND THIS MARRIAGE WAS TO CONCLUDE ENDLESS CIVIL WARS AND OLD HATREDS... HE WOULD NOT HAVE IT SO. LET IT BE AS HE WISHES -- I HAVE NEVER CROSSED THE PATH OF DESTINY. AND HE KNOWS THE FUTURE BETTER THAN I. IT IS POSSIBLE THAT NO EVENT IS WITHOUT MEANING.

HE HAS ALWAYS BEEN SO PRUDENT, SO SERIOUS AND SO STEADY... SINCE THE DEATH OF HIS WIFE, HE HAS LIVED SOLELY FOR HIS SON, YNIOLD. HE'S FORGOTTEN EVERYTHING. ...WHAT ARE YOU GOING TO DO?

WHO IS THERE ?

IS IT YOU, PELLEAS? COME CLOSER SO I CAN SEE YOU IN THE LIGHT.

I RECEIVED ANOTHER LETTER AT THE SAME TIME AS THE LETTER FROM MY BROTHER — A LETTER FROM MY FRIEND, MARCELLUS... HE IS DYING AND ASKS FOR ME TO COME. HE SAYS HE KNOWS THE EXACT DAY OF HIS DEATH... HE SAYS I CAN ARRIVE BEFORE IT, IF I WANT, BUT THAT THERE IS NO TIME TO LOSE.

YOU SHOULD WAIT A LITTLE WHILE... WE DON'T KNOW HOW YOUR BROTHER'S RETURN WILL AFFECT US. MOREOVER, ISN'T YOUR FATHER UPSTAIRS HERE, PERHAPS MORE SICK THAN YOUR FRIEND? COULD YOU CHOOSE BETWEEN A FATHER AND A FRIEND ?

TAKE CARE THAT THE LAMP IS LIT THIS EVENING, PELLEAS.

3

IT IS DARK
IN THE GARDENS.
AND WHAT FORESTS,
WHAT FORESTS
AROUND THE
CASTLE!

YES, THEY
ASTONISHED ME,
TOO, WHEN I FIRST
CAME HERE. THERE ARE
PLACES WHERE THE SUN
NEVER PENETRATES. BUT
YOU SOON GROW ACCUSTOMED...
A LONG TIME, A LONG TIME...
I HAVE LIVED HERE NEARLY
FORTY YEARS... LOOK TO
THE OTHER SIDE, YOU
WILL FIND THE LIGHT
FROM THE SEA.

I HEAR
NOISE
DOWN
BE-
LOW...

AH!
IT'S
PELLEAS
...HE
SEEMS
TIRED,
HAVING
WAITED
SO
LONG
FOR
YOU...

HE
HAS
NOT
SEEN
US.

I THINK HE HAS
SEEN US, BUT DOESN'T
KNOW WHAT HE
SHOULD DO...

PELLEAS!
PELLEAS!
IS IT
YOU?

YES!
I CAME
FROM
THE
SIDE
FACING
THE
SEA...

95

96

4 DON'T YOU KNOW WHERE I HAVE BROUGHT YOU?-- I COME HERE OFTEN TO SIT, AT NOON, WHEN IT IS TOO HOT IN THE GARDENS. IT'S STIFLING TO-DAY, EVEN IN THE SHADE.

OH! THE WATER IS CLEAR...

IT IS AS COOL AS THE WINTER. IT IS AN OLD ABANDONED WELL. IT WAS CONSIDERED TO HAVE MIRACULOUS POWERS-- IT HEALED THE BLIND-- IT IS STILL CALLED THE "BLIND MAN'S WELL."

DOES IT NO LONGER HEAL THE BLIND?

NOW THAT THE KING IS ALMOST BLIND HIMSELF, PEOPLE NO LONGER COME...

HOW LONELY IT IS HERE..., THERE IS NO SOUND.

THERE IS ALWAYS AN EXTRAORDINARY SILENCE...,YOU COULD HEAR THE WATER SLEEP...

I'D LIKE TO SEE THE BOTTOM OF THE WELL.

IT HAS NEVER BEEN SEEN-- IT MAY WELL BE AS DEEP AS THE SEA.

98

101

WHAT IS IT THEN? -- CAN'T YOU RECONCILE YOURSELF TO LIFE HERE? IS IT TOO SAD HERE? -- AND THE FOREST, THE ANCIENT FOREST WITH-OUT ANY SUNLIGHT. BUT WE COULD MAKE ALL THAT MORE PLEASANT IF YOU WISH. AND THEN, JOY CANNOT BE HAD EVERY DAY -- THINGS MUST BE TAKEN AS THEY ARE,,,

SAY SOMETHING,-- I WILL DO ANYTHING YOU WANT,,,

YES, IT'S TRUE,,, YOU NEVER SEE THE SKY,,, I SAW IT FOR THE FIRST TIME THIS MORNING,,,

IS THAT WHAT HAS CAUSED YOUR TEARS, MY POOR MELISANDE? IS IT ONLY THAT? YOU WEEP BE-CAUSE YOU CAN'T SEE THE SKY? COME NOW, YOU ARE TOO OLD TO WEEP OVER SUCH THINGS,,,

,,,AND IS IT NOT SUMMER NOW? YOU WILL SEE THE SKY EVERY DAY-- THEN, NEXT YEAR,,, COME, GIVE ME YOUR HAND, GIVE ME BOTH YOUR LITTLE HANDS. OH! THESE LITTLE HANDS THAT I COULD CRUSH LIKE FLOWERS,,,

--BUT WHERE IS THE RING I GAVE YOU?

THE RING ?

--YES! OUR WEDDING RING--WHERE IS IT ?

I THINK,,, I THINK IT HAS FALLEN,,, BUT I KNOW WHERE IT IS,,,

WHERE IS IT?

YOU KNOW,,, YOU KNOW THE CAVE BY THE SEA.

YES,,,

WELL, IT WAS THERE,,, IT MUST HAVE BEEN THERE ,,,YES, YES, I REMEMBER,,, I WENT THERE THIS MORNING, TO GATHER SEASHELLS FOR YNIOLD,,, THERE ARE SOME LOVELY ONES THERE,,, IT SLIPPED OFF MY FINGER,,, BUT THE TIDE WAS RISING,,, AND I HAD TO LEAVE BEFORE I COULD FIND IT.

103

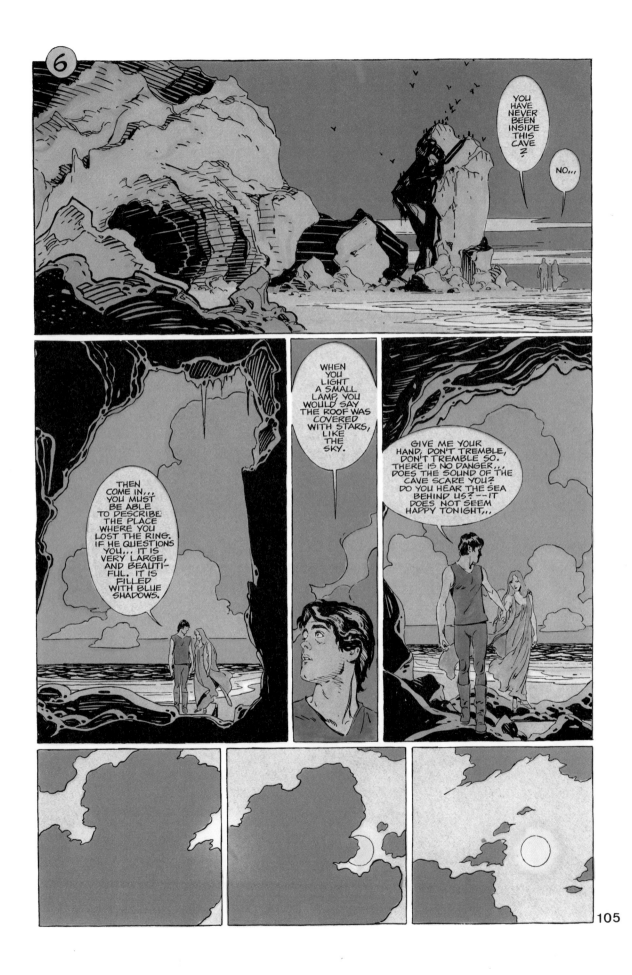

107

108

109

110

8

BE CAREFUL! THIS WAY! THIS WAY-- HAVE YOU NEVER DESCENDED INTO THESE VAULTS?

YES, ONCE, BUT THAT WAS LONG AGO.

WELL, HERE IS THE STAGNANT WATER I TOLD YOU ABOUT...

CAN YOU SMELL THE STENCH OF DEATH IN IT?

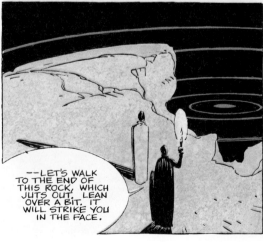

--LET'S WALK TO THE END OF THIS ROCK, WHICH JUTS OUT. LEAN OVER A BIT. IT WILL STRIKE YOU IN THE FACE.

LEAN OVER--DON'T BE AFRAID...

I WILL HOLD YOU...

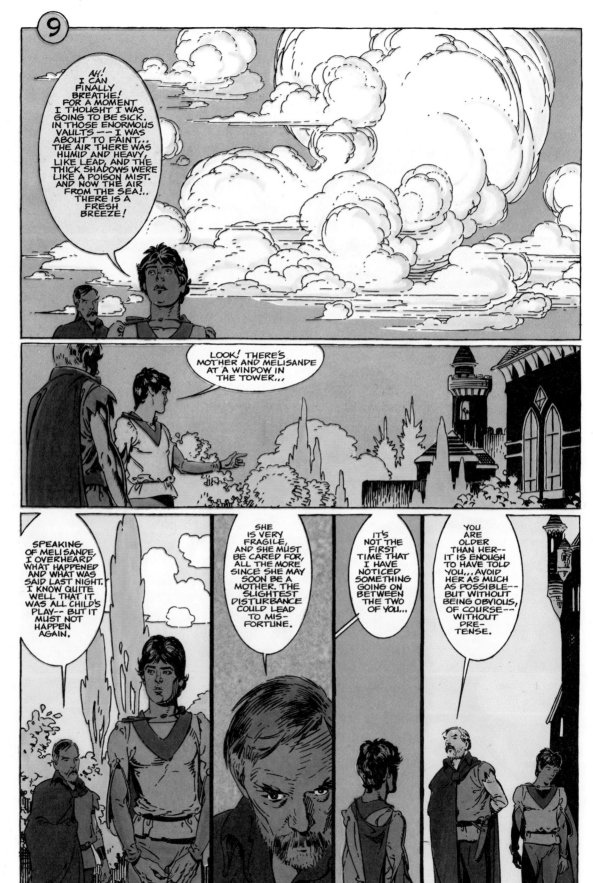

116

118

NOW THAT PELLEAS'S FATHER IS WELL, SOME JOY AND SUNLIGHT CAN FINALLY ENTER THE HOUSE... IT WAS TIME!

...FOR SINCE YOUR ARRIVAL, THERE HAS BEEN NOTHING BUT WHISPERING AROUND A CLOSED ROOM... TRULY, I PITIED YOU, MELISANDE...

I WATCHED YOU, YOU WERE THERE, HEEDLESS, PERHAPS, BUT WITH THE STRANGE AND DISTRACTED AIR OF SOMEONE WHO ALWAYS WAITS FOR SOME GREAT MISFORTUNE IN THE SUNLIGHT, IN A LOVELY GARDEN...

BUT IT MADE ME SAD TO SEE YOU-- FOR YOU ARE TOO YOUNG AND TOO BEAUTIFUL TO LIVE, DAY AND NIGHT, IN AN ATMOSPHERE OF DEATH...

BUT NOW ALL THAT WILL CHANGE. AT MY AGE, I HAVE LEARNED TO BELIEVE IN THE TRUTH OF EVENTS, AND I HAVE ALWAYS OBSERVED THAT YOUTH AND BEAUTY BRING WITH THEM YOUTHFULNESS, BEAUTY AND HAPPINESS... AND IT IS YOU WHO WILL NOW OPEN THE DOOR ON THE NEW ERA I HAVE PREDICTED...HOW I HAVE PITIED YOU THESE PAST MONTHS!

GRAND-FATHER, I HAVE NOT BEEN UNHAPPY...

LET ME LOOK AT YOU UP CLOSE, A MINUTE... SO CLOSE TO DEATH, ONE FEELS THE NEED FOR BEAUTY.

121

PELLEAS IS LEAVING TONIGHT.

YOU HAVE BLOOD ON YOUR FOREHEAD --WHAT HAS HAPPENED?

NOTHING, NOTHING... I CROSSED THROUGH A HEDGE OF THORNS.

LOWER YOUR HEAD, MY LORD... I WILL WIPE YOUR BROW...

I DON'T WANT YOU TO TOUCH ME, DO YOU UNDERSTAND? GO, GO AWAY! -- I WAS NOT SPEAKING TO YOU -- WHERE IS MY SWORD? -- I WAS LOOKING FOR MY SWORD...

HERE -- ON THE PRAYER STOOL.

BRING IT TO ME...

THEY HAVE JUST FOUND ANOTHER PEASANT, STARVED TO DEATH BY THE SEA. ONE WOULD THINK THEY ALL PLAN TO DIE BEFORE OUR EYES.

WELL, MY SWORD?

WHY ARE YOU TREMBLING SO? -- I AM NOT GOING TO KILL YOU. I SIMPLY WANT TO EXAMINE THE BLADE. -- I WOULD NOT USE THE SWORD FOR THAT.

WHY DO YOU LOOK AT ME LIKE A BEGGAR? -- I HAVE NOT COME BEGGING FOR ALMS. YOU'RE HOPING TO SEE SOMETHING IN MY EYES, WITHOUT MY SEEING ANYTHING IN YOURS? -- DO YOU THINK I KNOW SOMETHING?

123

124

THE LAST NIGHT... ALL MUST NOW END... LIKE A CHILD I HAVE BEEN PLAYING WITH SOMETHING I DID NOT FULLY UNDERSTAND... AS IN A DREAM, I HAVE PLAYED AMONG DESTINY'S TRAPS... WHAT HAS AWAKENED ME SO SUDDENLY? I SHALL FLEE, CRYING WITH JOY AND SADNESS, LIKE A BLIND MAN FLEEING A BURNING HOUSE... I SHALL TELL HER THAT I AM GOING TO ESCAPE.

IT IS LATE -- SHE HASN'T COME... IT WOULD BE BEST FOR ME TO LEAVE WITHOUT SEEING HER AGAIN... I WILL HAVE TO LOOK AT HER CAREFULLY THIS TIME... THERE ARE THINGS I NO LONGER REMEMBER... AT TIMES, YOU WOULD THINK I HAD NOT SEEN HER IN OVER A HUNDRED YEARS... AND I HAVE NOT YET LOOKED INTO HER EYES... I WILL HAVE NOTHING LEFT IF I LEAVE HER NOW. AND ALL THESE MEMORIES... IT'S AS IF I WERE CARRYING A FEW DROPS OF WATER IN A MUSLIN PURSE... I MUST SEE HER ONE LAST TIME, SEE INTO HER HEART...

I MUST SAY ALL THAT I HAVE NOT SAID TO HER...

PELLEAS!

127

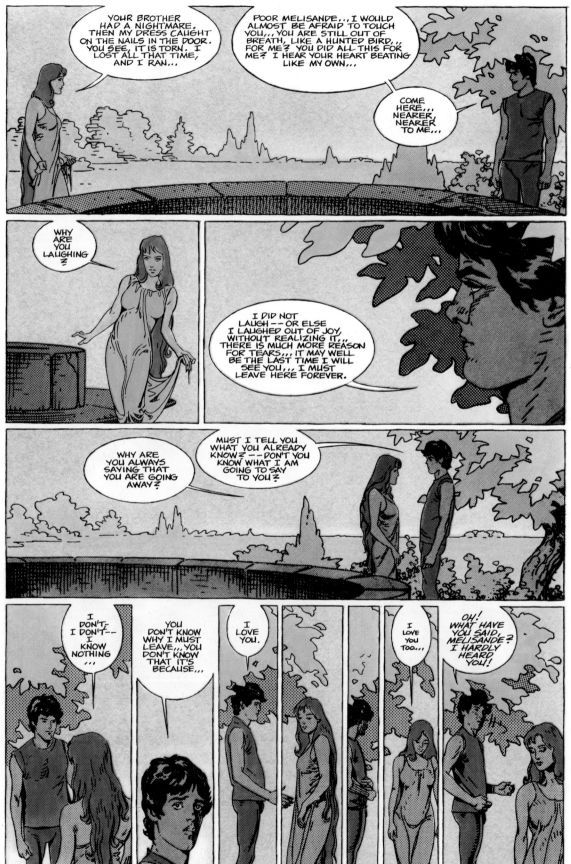

128

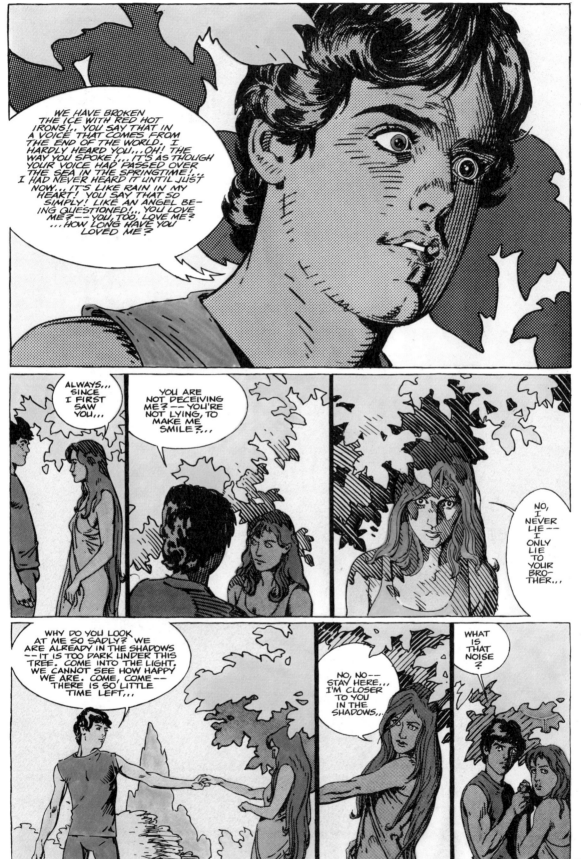

129

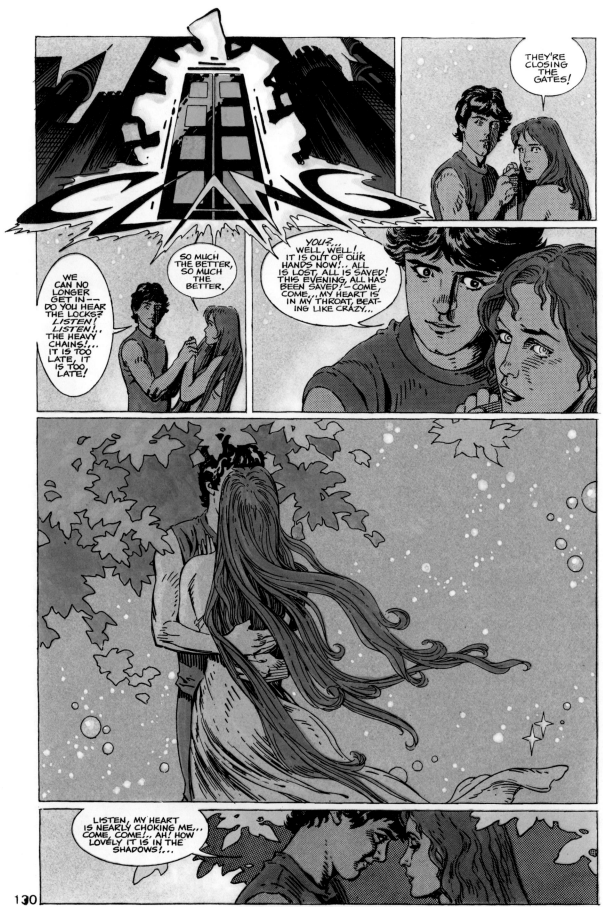

131

133

ISN'T THE SEA AIR TOO CHILLY TONIGHT?

DO IT, DO IT...

THANK YOU,,,IS THAT THE SUN SETTING?

YES, IT'S THE SUN SETTING ON THE SEA--IT'S LATE--THESE PAST FEW DAYS, YOU HAVE BEEN A LITTLE DELIRIOUS--YOU COULD NOT BE UNDERSTOOD...BUT NOW, ALL THAT IS PAST...HOW DO YOU FEEL, MELISANDE?

FINE, FINE-- WHY DO YOU ASK ME THAT? I HAVE NEVER FELT BETTER-- NEVERTHELESS, IT SEEMS THAT I KNOW SOMETHING...

WHAT ARE YOU SAYING? I DON'T UNDERSTAND YOU...

I DON'T KNOW,,, ARE YOU ALONE IN THE ROOM, GRANDFATHER?

NO, THE DOCTOR WHO CURED YOU IS STILL HERE,,,AND THERE IS ONE OTHER PERSON AS WELL,,,IT IS,,,DON'T BE AFRAID,,,HE DOES NOT WISH YOU ANY HARM,,, IF YOU ARE AFRAID, HE WILL LEAVE,,,HE IS VERY UNHAPPY,,,

WHO IS IT?

IT IS,,, IT IS YOUR HUSBAND,,, IT IS GOLAUD...

GOLAUD IS HERE? WHY DOESN'T HE COME NEAR?

MELISANDE,,, MELISANDE,,,

IS IT YOU, GOLAUD?,, I HARDLY RECOGNIZED YOU,,,IT MUST BE THE SETTING SUN IN MY EYES,,,WHY ARE YOU LOOKING AT THE WALLS? YOU HAVE GROWN SO THIN AND SO OLD,,, HAS IT BEEN SO LONG SINCE WE LAST MET?

WOULD YOU PLEASE LEAVE US ALONE FOR A MINUTE, MY FRIENDS,,,,I WILL LEAVE THE DOOR WIDE OPEN,,, ONLY FOR A MINUTE,,, I WOULD LIKE TO TELL HER SOMETHING -- OTHERWISE, I WOULD NEVER BE ABLE TO REST IN PEACE,,, WOULD YOU BE SO KIND? --YOU CAN COME BACK IMME- DIATELY,,,DON'T REFUSE ME THIS,,, I AM AN UNHAPPY MAN,,,

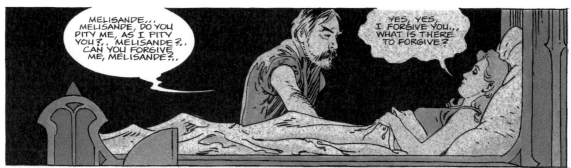

138

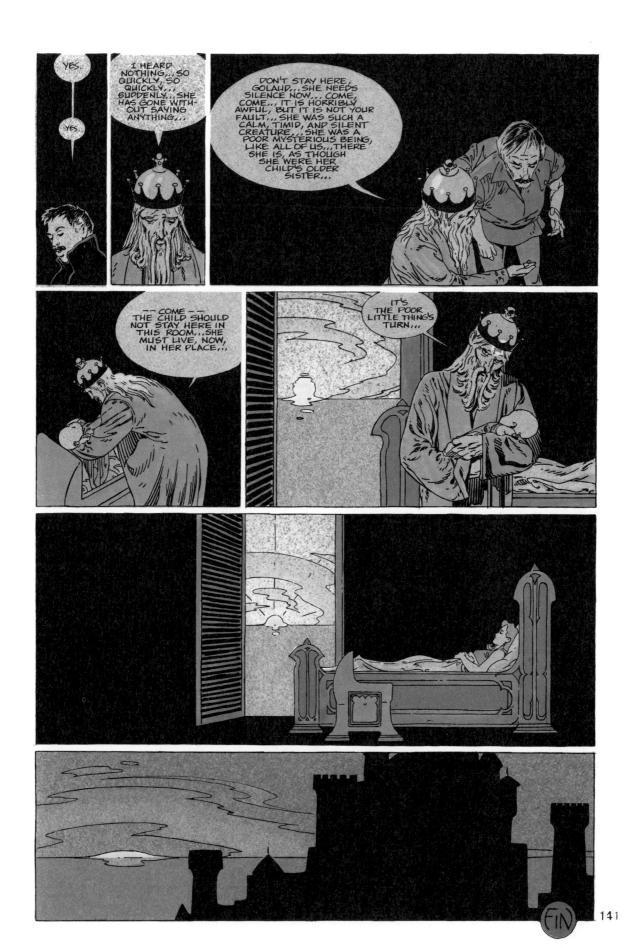

BIOGRAPHY

Philip Craig Russell was born on November 30, 1952, the thirteenth anniversary of Orson Welles' *War of the Worlds* broadcast. One wonders if there was a coincidence. Russell began his professional comics career in 1973. Having served his apprenticeship drawing stories featuring overly muscled superheroes, by 1976 Russell's art had taken on a more lyrical approach. He and a handful of other young artists each developed individualistic styles that set them apart from their peers. Whereas those few other artists left the comics field to produce portfolios and prints, Russell remained with comics. His reason? He believes comics to be a challenging storytelling medium and he is, first and foremost, a teller of stories. He has taught at Kent State University, and received a grant from the Ohio Arts Council for his comics adaptation of Rudyard Kipling's *Red Dog*, published by Eclipse Comics. P. Craig Russell lives in his native state of Ohio.

OTHER ECLIPSE ALBUMS

Sabre by Don McGregor and Paul Gulacy
The Rocketeer by Dave Stevens
The Sacred and the Profane by Ken Steacy and Dean Motter
Somerset Holmes by Bruce Jones, April Campbell, and Brent Anderson
Silverheels by Bruce Jones, Scott Hampton, and April Campbell
The Sisterhood of Steel by Christy Marx and Peter Ledger
Valkyrie, Prisoner of the Past by Charles Dixon, Paul Gulacy, and Willie Blyberg
Scout: The Four Monsters by Timothy Truman and Thomas Yeates
Heartbreak Comics by David Boswell
Alex Toth's Zorro by Alex Toth
Miracleman Book One by Alan Moore, Garry Leach, and Alan Davis
Real Love: The Best of the Simon and Kirby Romance Comics edited by Richard Howell
Pigeons from Hell by Robert E. Howard, adapted by Scott Hampton
Brought to Light by Alan Moore, Bill Sienkiewicz, Joyce, Brabner, Thomas Yeates, and Paul Mavrides
Teen-Aged Dope Slaves and Reform School Girls edited by Dean Mullaney
Bogie by Claude Jean-Philippe and Patrick Lesueur
Ariane and Bluebeard by Maurice Maeterlinck, adapted by P. Craig Russell
Into the Shadow of the Sun: Rael by Colin Wilson
Dr. Watchstop: Adventures in Space and Time by Ken Macklin
James Bond: Licence to Kill by Mike Grell, Richard Ashford, Chuck Austen, Tom Yeates, and Stan Woch
Tapping the Vein by Clive Barker, adapted by P. Craig Russell, Scott Hampton, John Bolton, Klaus Janson
Toadswart D'Amplestone by Tim Conrad
The Hobbit by J.R.R. Tolkien, adapted by Charles Dixon, Sean Deming, and David Wenzel
The Return of Valkyrie by Timothy Truman, Charles Dixon, Thomas Yeates, Stan Woch, and Will Blyberg
Scout: Mount Fire by Timothy Truman
Appleseed: The Promethean Challenge by Masamune Shirow
Larry Marder's Beanworld by Larry Marder
Tales of the Mysterious Traveler by Steve Ditko
Dirty Pair: Biohazards by Toren Smith and Adam Warren
What's Michael? by Makoto Kobayashi
Pogo by Walt Kelly
Krazy & Ignatz by George Herriman
Miracleman Book Two by Alan Moore, Alan Davis, Chuck Beckum, Rick Veitch, et al.

FOR A COMPLETE LIST OF 1,000 ECLIPSE GRAPHIC ALBUMS, COMIC BOOKS, TRADING CARDS, BOOKS, AND POSTERS
AVALIABLE BY MAIL, PLEASE SEND A SELF-ADDRESSED, STAMPED ENVELOPE TO
ECLIPSE BACK ISSUES, POST OFFICE BOX 1099, FORESTVILLE, CALIFORNIA 95436.